DON'T BE THE NEXT VICTIM

D1403735

Contents

DISCLAIMER AND TERMS OF USE AGREEMENT:

(Please Read This Before Using This Report)

Defining Identity Theft

Suppose you get robbed as you walk down the street, trying to get to your house. Suddenly out of nowhere, a person runs right to you, knocks you over and makes off with your wallet or purse and before you really register in your brain what has happened, they are gone.

Now what do you do? It is like a bad movie scene and it seems as if this type of crime will get worse and worse.

Why that may be you ask?

With this new technological age, thieves don't have to rob a person face to face, nor rob a bank and other establishments. Why? Getting the person's information in obtaining employment, credit and bank accounts and other ways to get money or credit, does this.

This activity, called Identity Theft, is so common that it has already affected millions of victims in the United States and Canada. Over the past few years, news stories about it have been reported. These stories make people aware of the crime. Also, campaigns and laws have been passing to build up the public's awareness as well as to combat the growing problem.

In September 2003, the Federal Trade Commission said that people who become victims of identity theft spend an average of $1,400 and close to 200 hours just cleaning up the damage to their personal and financial character.

The only catch is once this crime becomes more barefaced; the identity theft victim may spend more money and time just to clean up the issue. In terms of frustration, it's going to cost more than anyone thinks or even knows.

Identity Theft – Don't Be The Next Victim!

Should you be one of those unlucky ones that do not have the kind of money it would take to fix your credit record, you know what being a casualty of identity theft is all about. You know how you can become a victim and you know there are steps to fight against this terrible epidemic.

How does identity theft work? It's a crime which a person or group of persons use an individual's personal information. This means telephone number, name, phone card, credit card and social security number. It is done without the person's knowledge for criminal acts. Acts typically range from financial fraud or purchasing consumer goods by using their credit. This will leave the person to pay the bill unless they can prove it was not them that got the credit. Typically, until they look on their credit report or try to get loans, they will not know anything is wrong.

Although a serious crime, thieves, once they have the information, will commit at least eight different crimes in the victims' name. * make purchases or order goods without the * intention to pay

* apply for credit
* open bank accounts
* apply for loans
* apply for government benefits
* obtain cable or utility services using the another person's (victim) name
* forge checks or bank drafts * use victim's accounts to obtain money through wire transfers using the victim's accounts * and other similar acts of fraud.

Identity theft doesn't just apply toward individuals but also businesses… this is especially true for those of medium and limited businesses. It happens when a person applies for goods under a business' name.

People need to be active in not becoming an identity theft victim and make sure that all private documents and data are protected and not given into the wrong hands. Only through these steps can be stop ourselves from being a victim. It is important people stop the thieves before they strike.

How Does Identity Theft Happen?

Understanding identity theft protection is something that you should do. When you find something on your credit report or on your credit card statement, you may think to yourself, how did that happen? But, what you need to know is what to do to make sure that it does not happen. When you take the time to do this, you will find yourself in a better understanding of what could happen to you. Then, you can make sure that you do not see anything shocking on your reports down the road.

Identity theft happens in a number of ways. You don't have to actually hand out your information to anyone in order to have this happen to you. In fact, most people are not in this situation. Those that have had this happen to them generally have had it done without their actual input. For example, they may be paying for a meal at a restaurant. They trustingly hand over their credit card to the server to pay for their meal. Then, they go on their merry way. Yet, the problem here is that the waitress may have had the time to go to the workstation, jotted down your information on your credit card and then been able to use this information to make charges to your credit card.

Or, perhaps it was someone else that you handed your credit card information to. If you go in to talk to someone about having a home improvement project done and provide them with your address and then pay for an estimate, they instantly have everything that they need to use your credit card. Now, generally, it is not going to be the person that you hand your card over to, but perhaps it could be someone that is less than trustworthy working for them.

Many people think that credit card identity theft only happens on the web. The fact of the matter is, though, that you do not have to have this happen to you in this way. You face the same risk of identity theft on the web as you do in that restaurant. Trust is something that almost always plays a role though. In any case, learning how to protect yourself from these cases is your ultimate goal. Be sure to know when to spot someone that could potentially have the opportunity to gather your information, such as in these examples.

All The Different Methods Of Identity Theft

Although there are many different methods that one can utilize to rip someone off in an identity theft type scam, there are really only two basic types of actual identity theft. The first of these is generally the easiest and most basic way for thieves to achieve their objective. An example of Account takeover is when a thief gets hold of your actual physical credit card, or perhaps just the card number and expiry date, using it to purchase services or products. This works out extremely well for the thief, as the credit card owner doesn't usually notice the additional purchases until they either receive their monthly statement in the mail or have attempted to use the card and found that it has reached the maximum limit allowed.

The second type of identity theft is called Application fraud, or what is otherwise known as "true name fraud". In order for a thief to be successful at application fraud, they must have access to a good deal of your personal information such as your Social Security Number (SSN), full name, address, place of work, salary, driver's license number, date of birth etc. Of course not all of these pieces of information would be necessary for a thief to get away with application fraud but certainly a combination of some of the above would be required.

It Can Affect Anyone

Like many, you may assume that identity theft only happens to those people who might be a bit more careless when it comes to safeguarding personal information.

Or perhaps you are of the mindset that because you don't really have a lot of money in your personal account or don' have credit cards with large spending limits, that identity theft thieves wouldn't necessarily target someone like yourself. Well, make no mistake about it; identity theft can happen to anyone, including you! Basically, if you have an identity (and we hope that you do) then you are susceptible.

Are You Safe From Identity Theft?

Are you really safe from identity theft? Each day people are being attacked. So how would you feel if you got arrested for a crime you did not commit? The phone rings and creditors are harassing you saying you owe X amount of dollars despite the fact you do not have a credit card or you haven't used it in that month. What will you say to them?

Perhaps when you become a victim you will have the answers to these questions. But until then...

People say that identity theft is the "perfect crime" Everyone who is anyone can be a victim including children. The best way to prevent yourself from being the prey is learn about the crime. There are millions affected every year.

Once a thief decides to take your place in your life, it's almost impossible to get that life back. So you have not been a victim of ID theft, then do not take any risk that can harm those chances.

Identity Theft – Don't Be The Next Victim!

ID theft is the type of crime that one person pretends to be another in sake of getting information, money or any other reasons. This is typically done for financial reasons and or criminal activity.

Information that the thieves look to get are the potential victim's complete name, their date of birth and any array of related data such as social security number, passport, driver's license number and credit card number.

Once the thief has any part of the information, he or she can use it to take over the victim's accounts. He or she can apply for loans and even purchase items and services.

The thief can also apply for medical benefits, education assistance and other personal finances. Just by creating or forging birth certificates or immigration documents, all this can be gotten when presented to the right agency that provides this type of help.

For those who are involved in this kind of crime either wants to mislead police on who is committing the fraud or hide from police while they are pursuing the assailant. Some like to use the person's name to do larger crimes and do human trafficking and terrorism acts.

According to the Federal Trade Commission (FTC) 29 percent of complaints come from individuals from people aged 18-29, 25 percent for 30-39 individual ages, 21 percent in from individuals in their 40s. 13 percent from the individuals in 50s. The remaining 10 percent come from those ages 60 and older.

Thieves target those who have an average income and those with good credit.

Do not forget that even children can be victims of identity theft especially from their relatives...their parents mainly.

Even businesses, corporations and smell enterprises can be struck by identity theft by thieves disguising themselves as the top executives of the company. They withdrawal large sums of money which can topple business relations and its reputation.

This day and age, ID theft can be committed by gaining access to information systems and duplicating, although not the original, important documents. Afterwards, they can open new credit accounts and charging older ones.

Technological advances have made it possible for hackers to break into public databases and cracking important government sites.

There are seven ways to guard yourself from these thieves though not altogether foolproof.

- Make sure to never provide your Social Security number unless it is required;

- Shred important documents;

- Checks should only have your name and address;
- Carry only necessary documents needed for the day;
- Review credit reports regularly. Look for unauthorized accounts;
- Never give out private data on the phone.

Why Is Identity Theft Protection So Important?

If you are a user of credit cards, then you probably know why identity theft protection is important. In short, if you allow someone else to get your credit information, they can easily take that information and build a large pile of credit card debt that will affect you for a long time. There is no easy way out of this problem either.

Depending on the seriousness of the amount of debt that is piled up against you, you could be spending countless days trying to work through it all. In the end, if you do not have the right identity theft protection in place, you may actually find yourself in a lot of trouble.

If you were to become a victim of identity theft in which someone else took your personal information and used it to gain access to credit, it is very hard to prove that this really was not you that did it. You will need to go through a long list of things including talking to your lenders, the lenders that have files against you that you may not actually have had, and a wide range of other things. You may end up having to pay an attorney to get the whole thing figured out too. It simply is not worth all this trouble when you can just use tools to help you to safeguard against this.

Let's say that someone had the opportunity to use your credit card. Let's just say that they got it from your wallet and you have had no idea. They can easily go from place to place in a matter of minutes, charge up a lot of debt at various stores and other locations and walk away with all of that merchandise. It may take them just a few hours to do this. In the meantime, you have no idea that you do not even have your credit card. If this happens, your identity theft protection on your credit card should kick in for you. In some cases (the better credit lenders) if they see a lot of spending on your credit card at once they may put a hold on it in order to contact you before allowing additional charges.

But, let's say that they do clear it all up for you. This is still not the end to your problems. More than likely, you are still going to have problems. Your credit card may put a limit on the amount of transactions on your account to safeguard themselves from this happening again. This means that you are limited for something that someone else did to you. Having identity theft protection and using it is very important to your well-being, in many respects.

What Is Identity Theft Protection?

Identity theft is a very troublesome occurrence for those that happen to have to deal with it. The sad note here is, though, that many times, you will not know what hit you when it does happen. While protection from identity theft is the most important thing for you to know, you also need to understand what this term means and just how it can happen to you. Unfortunately, many individuals, thousands each year, will experience some form of identity theft.

Protection from identity theft starts by understanding just what it is. This term is used loosely to represent several things. First, there are those instances where an individual will literally pose as you. This is the most intense type of identity theft and also the hardest to pull off. Yet, it is also one of the least common types out there.

The most common type of identity theft is that of those individuals that will use your personal information to gain something for themselves, such as a credit card or, even worse, they will use the credit cards that you have opened for their needs. Identity theft protection is mostly about being aware and taking the time to really know what you are doing when you had out your information. It is also important to be able to spot when something is happening to you.

Some of those that are victims of identity theft will not know about it until it is too late to do anything about it. Yet, it is easy for to you to catch something long before it gets to that serious of an issue.

For example, if someone got a hold of your credit card information, you may think it would take you a month or more to know about it. Yet, if you manage your finances online, you can easily check out your credit card statement (with most banks) online without much hassle.

If you do this just once a week, you can help to protect yourself.

There are many forms of identity theft and sometimes, there is not much that you can do to protect yourself from it. Yet, being a smart consumer is the first step. You should always know what should be on your credit cards and you should know what is on your credit report. If you do not know this, you are likely going to have to unwrap quite a tangled mess later on. Being a smart consumer is necessary here.

ID Theft Scams

It can be said a person should be proud to be the only person born with their identity. You are unique, given a name by your proud parents. You work hard for the monies in your account. You should expect plenty of benefits from your SSS when you reach retirement age.

Yet, some people feel it necessary to steal your hard worked earnings by taking on your identity. How would you feel by this? What would your life be like then? No doubt all these bring a fear that someone will damage your reputation, your life and your security.

Many people don't want to grow old without some kind of security but everyone must work together to keep identity thieves from getting what they want. These thieves don't deserve a cent for their hacker time.

People are starting to fight back. They are beginning to demand their government to secure their identities more carefully. If identity theft wasn't so prevalent, then there would be no reason for this.

Identity theft is a grave miscarriage of justice for people affected because their personal information and property were compromised. It is only right that they seek justice to combat this growing epidemic.

Identity Theft – Don't Be The Next Victim!

Every precaution should be taken to protect people's identity. Once this is done, thieves can do little to steal it from you. This can make people take a little comfort that no one can be them.

No doubt if the person behind the first attack of identity theft were ever found, people would want to seek justice behind their stealing abilities. Many people would want that person to suffer as they have suffered.

From one person to a group of people to many others, identity theft and all the fraud that come with it has no doubt fanned out. The FBI or rather the Federal Bureau of Investigations has found it harder than easier to get rid of this problem.

Since the thieves have been able to stay one step ahead of the authorities, it makes it harder for the FBI agents to track them down.

Not only that, but the fraud is growing rapidly on the Internet. Should you be looking to buy a high priced item on a website, be sure to investigate it to see if it is legit or not.

Some of his fraudulent websites will offer the products, like IPods or high end cell phones, at a drastic reduced cost or close to free.

When a person is trying to scam someone, they advise people not to pay for anything until they receive the product. However, what will happen is they will take the name of the person buying and take it from the account of another to purchase the prize from the legit site.

Basically, once the person pays for the item, the money is transferred to the thief. The scammer can still present a copy of the receipt to the buyer although the money is coming from another account number.

E-mail fraud is also running rampant. What is this type of fraud? When an e-mail is sent to you from a scammer, they often times place a link. The e-mail would seem as if it is coming from a place of business that you contend with on a regular basis.

The scammer will ask for all kinds of information including social security number, full name, mother's maiden name and your date of birth.

Are you starting to understand how this type of fraud works? So before you fall victim, take precautions early to avoid being a prey to those thieves.

Put An End To Criminal Identity Theft

If you are mistakenly identified as somebody else, it can get you into a lot of trouble if that person were a criminal right? Imagine the vice versa is true for a criminal. If he takes on your identity life is much easier for him! No harm done? Not until he commits a crime again, and then YOU are the one who will be called in for questioning.

How it's done: *The criminal of modern day has made use of technology to get personal information in a very subtle way. A hacker, if he has access to your mail id, can probably get your bank information and your social security number from there. Using these he or she could start a new bank account under your name, get a credit card under your name and even make a driver's license in your name. Imagine now, how vulnerable we all are to these hackers. The bad guy uses all your personal information to establish a new and verified identity of his (yours!). Using this identity he may commit crimes like online harassment to other people, obscene phone calls from a number listed to you, and sometimes even robbery and murder. Finally the police end up on the wrong trail and come knocking at the wrong door. Needless to say the judicial system is efficient* *enough not to punish the wrong man, but the guilty gets away scot free, and by this time he is probably using a different identity to cover his tracks.*

Imagine a guy with a fake driver's license (in your name) being stopped for something like over speeding. He escapes the fine by leaving his (yours) driving license number with the police.
He doesn't show up at court and the summon is sent to your doorstep. And you are left wondering what you did!

Criminal identity theft is exactly what these examples tell you it is. It is the theft of your identity for criminal usage. It is definitely a personal crime, and directly affects the person whose identity is being used - sooner or later he or she will be in trouble for something they never did. If you feel that your identity may be under threat of theft, or if you are suspicious of it having happened here are a few ideas for you -

The first thing you should think of doing is the obvious. Call the cops, and tell them why you think your identity is being used by an imposter. B. You need to fill out a convincing report about the impersonation incident. Think clearly and objectively while filling out the report, it is what will help the officials track down the guilty.

Get a lawyer if the matter turns serious or if you are unsure of the state laws.

What Are The Effects Of Identity Theft On An Organization?

Imagine the damage to an organization if identity thieves stole their information like individuals. It is beyond comprehension and likely to be more damaging reputation wise.

Identity Theft – Don't Be The Next Victim!

No doubt thieves love to steal people's hard earned cash. To them, it's like they dug a hole and struck oil. Since the benefits seem to outweigh the risks, they continue to do it more and more.

With the Internet's popularity and computer databases, this has been the dessert that identity thieves have been waiting for. This is the way many thieves obtain their information about their victims.

Both the social and economic effects of this crime should not be ignored. If those who do not have much and are not known throughout the world can be scammed and victimized, then big organizations have more to lose if they get preyed on.

While there's no perfect outcome, each organization that wants to stay afloat should take precautions against identity theft.

When identity thefts in organizations occur, it is because of two specific reasons: Negligence and lenient standards.

How does an organization fail in negligence? It can be as simple as not checking the background of people they are selling their information to. Some companies are not aware that this is how many identity thieves get the information they need.

When companies carry around their information on portable devices or gadgets such as laptops or notebooks, this is just asking for trouble. It is a convenient way for companies to keep up with the data they need. However, company personnel need to keep up with these devices at all times.

Oddly enough, owners do no protect or encrypt any of the information they have stored. Not doing these results in the identity thieves' access to personal and organization related data.

It is has been reported that bigger organizations have lost data for their company or about their customers. There are two reasons for this.

First, the company may not have the resources to adequately store big files. Second, they have no ways of knowing what employees could be doing and what their employees have access to.

Thieves use state of the art tactics

Many company attacks have been done as a result of: a weakness in computer hardware or software. This is especially true for problems that occur in operating systems, firewalls, web browsers, or even internal processing software. All this to gain access to data that would otherwise be private.

How can these be fought off?

Organizations can use up to date security software updates. When a system is left vulnerable, working with a known weakness, identity thieves jump on this opportunity.
Senior security management need to handle fast and efficiently a company's weaknesses to stave off any threat of identity theft.

Each company needs to know where their customer data is going. This is called data flow mapping. This helps company managers to track the information and see who has access to this data.

Proof needs to be collected when an incident occurs. It is important that the company gathers the evidence or else not doing so can make it severely impossible to track criminals.

Tracking it could also give the organization civil compensation. Hiring a person who is qualified to be a "forensic technology scientist" is a smart plan for the organization.

Organizations and their employees should never take for granted that because they are too large that they will not be affected. This is exactly the opposite. Like individuals, companies should protect themselves as much as possible if not more.

How To Prevent Identity Theft

Let's check in to see how you're doing before we go any further. That was a lot of information to absorb and for someone who's new to the whole world of Identity Theft it was likely very overwhelming.

You're doing really well though and I'm proud of you! You made it through the most difficult part of this book. You learned all about the scariness of ID theft and the many forms it can take and look, you're still here. Now it's time for your reward. The first portion of this book may have caused you to feel helpless, frightened or without power against the enormity of the problem. Now however it's time for you to learn that there is something you can do about it. Knowledge is power and here is where you become EMPOWERED!

Protecting Your Mail Remember how we talked about thieves that would steal your mail from the garbage and even from your own mailbox? Well don't let them! Make sure that every single piece of mail with any kind of identifying information on it is shredded before you throw it away. Simply tearing it into a few pieces is not adequate protection.

This only provides the thief with a fairly basic jigsaw puzzle to your most valued information. Invest in a small shredder for your home. These are very inexpensive especially when you consider that the minimal cost of the item could save you hundreds or thousands of dollars in the long run, not to mention a huge headache. If you can't purchase one yourself then take your mail to work with you and use the shredder in your office.

A locked mailbox will not completely guarantee your protection from identity thieves but it certainly may help in dissuading their attempts to steal your mail. Look into purchasing a mailbox that has a slot in the top for the mail to be slid into but where you need a key to actually remove it.

This way, if your mailbox is broken into you will at least know it right away and will perhaps be able to notify creditors, banks and other companies before any real damage is done.

Identity Theft Protection: What To Do Now

Identity theft protection is something that you need to know and take care of every single day. Each day, you make choices about your identity mainly with the use of your credit card. If you are one of the people that realize just how easy it is for someone to get a hold of your information, then you know that it is up to you to make sure that they do not get the information that is going to ruin your credit score and put your life at a full stop. Here is what you need to do now in order to make sure that you have the highest level of protection possible.

•Make sure that you have identity theft protection on your credit cards. To know this, call and talk to your credit card lenders. Some may offer a better protection policy for a different type of credit card. When you apply for a new card, always insure that you get this protection on it.

•Get a copy of your credit report and insure that everything on it is correct. This should include your address and your account information. Take a look at who is inquiring about your credit as well. Make sure that you clear up any discrepancies that are listed there as well.

•Use spyware on your computer. If you connect to the internet with your pc, then you need to have updated spyware on your computer. This will help to monitor anyone that tries to apply a program that could be used to track what you are doing online as well as record information that you enter there and then report it back to a thief. Make sure to run a complete scan at least weekly as well.

•Check your balances. You should know how much you are using on your credit cards and you should know when there are not charges that you are familiar with. A good option to make sure that this happens is to have an online account set up with your credit card companies.
This way, you can easily check your transactions daily or at least weekly to insure that everything is okay.

When you take the time to insure that your information is protected, you can insure that your credit and your identity are safe. Taking the time to check out this information takes only minutes but it can save you from many, many heartaches and costly expenses down the road.

Identity Theft Protection: What To Know And Do

When it comes to identity theft protection, it is up to you to get the best results possible. While there are plenty of things that you blame on someone else to do, it is really up to you to insure that you keep your personal information, especially your finances, in order.

To do this, though, there are many things that can help you. In fact, if you get into a routine it can be easy to make sure that your identity is always safe and secure. What you need first, though, is information.

In order to insure that you are protected, it is essential that you take the time to know how you can be affected by identity theft. For example, do you know how a thief can get your credit card number or information? If not, then you should educate yourself on that. Second, you should know what is available to help you in that protection. For starters, you should insure that you have identity theft protection available on your credit cards. This is a service that many credit cards offer that will help you to insure that if your credit gets lost or stolen that you are not responsible for the charges.

The next thing to do is to learn about your credit report. You need to be able to get your credit report and check it for any errors. You should do this at least once per year. If you are really adamant about your credit score and your credit history, you may want to purchase a credit monitoring program that can help you to be notified of new accounts as they appear on your credit report. All in all, it is up to you to make sure that the information that is provide about you is accurate.

How Did It Happen To Me?

For many people, the fact that their identity has been stolen is something that they just cannot believe. How did this happen to me?
The question is something that haunts people. But, what they do not know is that there were probably things that they could have done as identity theft protection. Now, that is not to say that everyone that is affected by identity theft can protect it, but many can.

To know what you can do to prevent identity theft from happening to you, there are several things that you need to learn about. Here are some of the things that you can do to make sure that it does not happen to you.

•Keep an eye on your credit card balances and make sure that you do not allow anyone that should not have them to get a hold of your credit card numbers and info. They can easily make payments without the credit card in hand with this information.

•Only use secure websites when it comes to making purchases on the web. A secure website is one that has an 'S' after the http in the browser's address box (the box you would type in website name into.) This is nearly an impossible situation for others to steal from.

•Never provide your personal information to anyone including your last name, your address or your credit card numbers. You should guard your social security number closely.

•Only purchase from reliable merchants on the web that you know. If you do not know the merchant, you may want to consider using an alternative form of payment. There are services online that allow you to pay through them so that your credit card information or bank account information is not at risk.

By doing these things, you can help to insure that your credit card information is not being used in the wrong way. Identity theft protection is something that you deserve to have.

Identity Theft Protection: Protecting Your Own Way

When it comes to identity theft protection, it is up to you to make sure that it gets done the way that it needs to be done. You should not count on your credit card companies letting you know that someone is using your credit card.

In fact, you could go months without realizing it and by then, it is far too late to have this taken care of. But, there are several things that you can do now to insure that you are going to have the best results when it comes to your identity.

Here's a look at the ways that you can have the best Identity theft protection.

- •*Always monitor your credit card statements for purchases that you did not make.*

- •*If you lose your credit card, report it as soon as possible to the lender so that it can be canceled and a new one listed. Review with the representative the charges that are on your card to insure that no one has used it.*

- •*Pull your credit report. You can do this for free once per year or pay for it more often. Consider a credit report monitoring program that will help you to know as soon as a new account is opened and when things are changed on your report.*

- •*Make sure that your credit cards have identity theft protection programs on them to help to safeguard against possible charges that you do not make.*

- *Make online purchases carefully. Make sure you are on a secure websites that you are using your credit card with a merchant that you know and trust and consider using payment services that allow for your information to be kept from the merchants that you do not know.*

- *Never provide your personal and financial information to anyone on the web that is not a legitimate business.*

Identity theft protection starts with you. You need to monitor it and you can when you use these services.

How To Avoid Identity Theft: Keeping Your Financial Records Safe

Imagine this scene: You're opening your bills, only to find one of your credit card account balances with an over-due five-digit charge. You know you didn't make that purchase, so you refuse to pay for it.

A few months later, you decide to buy a new car, so you submit a loan application to the car dealer. You get a phone call that afternoon with the bad news, "I'm sorry, Ms. Jones, but we are not able to extend credit to you at this time." When you ask why, they tell you that your credit report indicated you're in debt way over your ability to pay. Bummer! You've become a victim of identity theft.

Now imagine this: You finally order that credit report, like you've been meaning to do for years. When you get it, you learn that you own a house you don't know about and you have credit card balances at three different stores you've never even heard of. Someone has stolen your identity to make their life richer! How did the identity theft happen? And what can you do about it?

There are many ways an identity thief can get your personal information to build a mountain of debt that creditors expect you to pay. Maybe they got hold of your name, address, and social security number by going through your garbage one night. Or perhaps you gave them the information when "their representative" contacted you to verify some details on your account.

Or maybe they're a computer hacker that figured out how to get your credit card numbers when you made a purchase at the local boutique.

They may even have gotten your information by pretending to be you (or someone in your family) when they contacted your bank or service company. The worst-case scenario is when someone uses your social security number and then goes out and commits criminal acts.

Ever seen the inside of a police station or jail? You could! There are multitudes of ways to become a victim of identity theft!

Identity theft and fraudulent use of personal financial records is a growing problem all over the world. In 2004, the U.S. Federal Trade Commission conducted a study that indicated over 9 million people are victims of identity theft every year. A 2003 study conducted in the United Kingdom suggested that 20% of all consumers had been subject to identity theft. Clearly, in the English-speaking world, identity theft is an ever-greater threat to your personal and financial well-being.

How Can I Prevent Having My Identity Stolen?

Here are some tips on things you can do (or not do) to guard your personal financial information, prevent identity theft, and protect your good credit rating.

- Always take your receipts with you after you've made a purchase. Leaving the receipt at the ATM or gas station is an open invitation for identity thieves.

- Maintain good files and records of your financial transactions. Know what you've purchased, when, and from whom. Store your old account statements in a safe place. And be sure to shred any papers with personal information before you throw it away.

Identity Theft – Don't Be The Next Victim!

- *The FBI recently reported that a third of identity theft victims admitted the thief was a co- worker or friend. Be careful not to leave personal information out in the open on your desk or in your home office. And don't ask anyone else to hold your personal papers for you. In this case, most of the identity theft suspects were well aware of their victim's habits and lifestyle.*

- *Carefully guard your User IDs and passwords for online accounts. When you create them, don't go for the easy-to-remember. People who know you may be able to guess simple, straightforward user IDs and passwords. And don't write your passwords down or keep them where someone can get to them. If you store them electronically, make sure the files are protected.*

- *Get and keep regular copies of your credit reports and account statements. Use one or all of the three major agencies (Experian, TransUnion, or Equifax) to get your credit report. Don't depend on less reputable reporting agencies.*

- *Opt out of mailing lists whenever you can, and ask telemarketers to "take your name off their list." By law, they can't call you again for a year. If you have any doubts, check with your bank and credit accounts to find out what they do with your personal information and what you need to do to better protect it.*

- *Don't have printed or write your social security number on your checks. Might as well send it up a flag. Some states still use social security numbers for driver's licenses, but they are changing. Check with your DMV to see if you can have your driver's license changed to remove your social security number.*

- *Don't keep a written list of your bank or other account numbers where they might be seen by someone else. Keep lists of this type of information under lock and key.*

- Do not respond to and delete any e-mails that ask for an account number or other personal information. Stop internet and snail-mail credit card offers. Install firewall and anti-spyware on your computer for additional protection. If your computer has the feature, register your fingerprint as an additional safety feature.

- Purchase new checks from the bank, not a discount service. And rather than having your full name printed on the checks, use your initial.

- Do not carry PINs in your wallet or purse, and never give them out over the phone. What If I'm Already a Victim?

If you think someone else is using your identity or personal financial information inappropriately, contact the nearest office of the U.S. Department of Justice. Contact your creditors to alert them to the fraud. Also inform your bank of the activity and secure their agreement to help protect your information. You may want to revisit the names of people authorized to access your personal financial information and limit it to essential parties only.

Find out as much as you can about the accounts, purchases, and applications the identity thief has made using your name. Then contact those companies directly and immediately to make sure they close the accounts and notify law enforcement when they become aware of any additional transactions.

Immediately notify the credit reporting agency and creditors if you see suspicious activity or if you find errors like a closed account that shows as open or a paid-off balance that appears to be outstanding. You may have to provide documentation to support corrections, and you may have to make the same contact several times to assure the correction is made. But be persistent. Your credit report is a direct reflection of your financial dealings. Creditors and credit report agencies are obligated to report correct information.

Fifteen Easy Solutions To Avoid Being A Victim Of Identity Theft

Identity theft occurs when a criminal steals personal information from you. It may be your full legal name, your credit card or bank account numbers, your social security or driver's license number, or other personal data that identifies you uniquely. The identity thief uses the information to apply for mortgages, loans, or credit card applications under your name. They may even use the information to access your bank accounts.

This modern crime is rampant today, and public concerns about it continue to rise. While perpetrators of identity theft are difficult to catch and prosecute, here are a few things you can do to protect your personal financial information and avoid becoming a victim to this malicious crime:

1. Don't give your personal information to anyone over the phone. Callers who ask for your birth date or social security or other account numbers over the telephone are likely to be identity thieves looking for an easy mark.

2. Don't send this information to anyone through e-mail or snail mail unless you initiated contact and know and trust the person or company you're sending the information to.

3. Tear up or shred papers (like your mail) that have personal information on them before you throw them away. This applies to bank accounts, credit card statements, and unsolicited or pre- approved credit card applications.

4. Keep an accurate, up-to-date record (under lock and key) of all your account numbers, noting contact information if they should be lost or stolen. If they are lost, contact the company immediately to notify them and stop all transactions on the account. Be sure to record the service order or confirmation number of your report for later follow-up.

5. Unless you are using your credit cards, store them in a safe, locked place where no one can get to them without your knowledge.

Store unused checks, your social security card, and your bank and investment statements in a secure location.

6. Keep copies of your purchase receipts and make sure you got the card back when you used it.

7. Monitor your credit report regularly, at least once a year. By law, you can order one free credit report each year. The major companies that you should contact are Equifax, TransUnion, and Experian. Review the reports careful to assure you are aware of all accounts they include and that the information about the account status is correct and up-to-date. Be sure to check the section listing recent credit checks, and be sure you know why the inquiry was made.

8. When you are withdrawing money from an ATM, be sure there is no one standing behind you who can watch you enter your PIN.

9. Make sure no one can hear you if you give your credit card numbers or banking information to someone over the phone.

10. When make a purchase on the internet, be sure the website and your transaction are secure.

11. Install personal security measures on your PC. Use firewalls, virus protection, and adware to identify and remove unwanted cookies and spyware.

12. Password protect all of your internet accounts. Don't use easy-to-guess passwords like your birth date, phone number, or anniversaries. Change your passwords, at the least, every six months.

Use a mix of letters, numbers, and symbols that people are unlikely to figure out. NEVER give your password to someone else unless you are completely comfortable with them accessing your accounts.

13. If you do have to write your passwords down to remember them, keep them under lock and key, and don't share the information with anyone. If you keep them in a computer file, use password protection to discourage spying eyes.

14. Be very suspicious of calls from your bank or other institutions. They do not ask for personal information over the phone or by e-mail. Ask if you can call back or simply refuse to respond.

15. Get on one of the internet lists that remove your name from all pre-approved credit mailing lists. When telemarketers call, tell them to "Take my name off your list." By law, they can't call you again for a year.

16. Don't leave your mail in your personal or post office mailbox for extended periods. This is an open invitation to the identity thief.

17. Order your new checks from your bank and pick them up personally rather than having them mailed to you.

18. Consider purchasing an identity theft insurance policy.

19. To be alerted if someone attempts to make credit applications or transactions under your name, register at a credit watch company that will routinely check your credit report for you on a regular basis and inform you when something in your report has changed. You can also purchase this service from the major credit reporting companies.

20. If you think you may be a victim of identity theft, report it immediately to the U.S. Justice Department and your local police. Also notify your credit card companies and the three credit report agencies to prevent further transactions under your name. Ask credit report companies to freeze your credit report by making a request via certified mail. They will not charge you the normal $10 fee if you are a victim of identity theft.

What Can I Do To Prevent Identity Theft Before It Happens?

To avoid becoming a victim of identity theft, follow these guidelines:

1. Keep a very close eye on your credit card activities. Check statements closely as soon as you receive them, and confirm that you made or approved all of the purchases. If there are questionable charges on your statement, contact the company immediately to find out when and where the purchase was made and to formally dispute the charge. You might be surprised to know how many people fail to review their statements carefully each month. Failure to attend to your accounts could leave you thousands, even hundreds of thousands, in debt with no products or services to show for it.

2. Request credit report updates at least twice a year. Look for a lower-than-expected credit score, unfamiliar accounts, or credit inquiries from companies you don't do business with.

3. Be careful to protect your personal financial papers. Keep them in a secure location, preferably under lock and key. And don't allow other people to access them without your express permission.

4. Be alert when you're writing checks or using your ATM card. Is there anyone near enough who could read and steal personal information or your PIN number? Be careful to protect these items from view.

5. Deliver your bill payments directly to the post office, and don't let your mail sit in your mail box too long. This is an open invitation to the ever-vigilant identity thief.

6. Use unexpected and unique passwords on all your internet accounts, mixing letters with numbers and symbols. And change your passwords at least every six months.

Keep up on the news about new identity theft strategies and scams. Read the paper and surf the internet to find out who's doing what these days. Make sure you know what your creditors do with their customers' personal information and demand they protect it.

Avoid becoming a victim of identity theft by applying common sense and careful thought to your everyday transactions. Question people who ask for inappropriate information and feel empowered to refuse to answer. Remember that you may not know your co-workers and acquaintances very well. Do not share your information with anyone you don't trust 100%.

Ways On Preventing Identity Theft

Identity theft has become the crime of the 21st Century. Criminals steal personal information from others and then "pose" as their victim to secure mortgages and loans, open new credit or make purchases on existing accounts, or even access their victim's bank accounts to steal their money.

It's difficult to control identity theft. First, it's hard to know when it's happening. Second, because the thief is using a false identity, it's hard to catch and prosecute them.

Identity Theft – Don't Be The Next Victim!

Federal and state governments are doing what they can to prevent identity theft by passing new legislation identifying it as a crime worthy of prison time and then trying to enforce the laws. Businesses are developing and installing better security on their computer systems and trying harder to protect their customers' personal information from hackers.

But, at least in today's world, preventing identity theft falls largely upon us, the individual consumer.

Here are some tips to help you protect yourself from this malicious, damaging crime: Here are some ways to prevent identity theft:

1. Protect your mail with a lock

Whether using your residential mail box or renting a box at the Post Office or postal service, be sure your mail is protected from the eyes and hands of greedy criminals. Stealing mail that contains personal information is perhaps the biggest source of identity theft today.

2. Rent a box from your Post Office or a postal service

Especially if you're frequently away from home, you'll enjoy better personal security if you keep your mail where others have their eyes on it when you're away. And you can let the service know who is authorized to open your mailbox if necessary. Keep the key with you, and don't lend it to people you're not sure about. Use this service for posting your outgoing mail as well. Don't leave it attached to your residential mailbox where anyone can pick it up. Finally, ask the Post Office to hold your mail while you're gone on long trips. It will be much more secure at the post office than in your mailbox.

3. NEVER give out personal information over the phone.

Some identity thieves pose as representatives for a charity or a telemarketing or polling firm to fool you into trusting them enough to get your personal information. Don't even give your birth date to them!
Ask if you can call them back. Better yet, simply hang up. You don't owe these callers a thing!

4. Have a private, unlisted phone number

You'll be more secure if the only people who know your number got it directly from you. And give your phone number to those people you trust. Ask them not to share it with others unless they ask you first. You have a right to your privacy. Don't use the unlisted number on internet or printed forms either. And if you do get calls from telemarketers, tell them to "Take my name off your list." By law, they can't call you again for a year when you make this request.

5. Keep your PINs and passwords in a safe place

If you don't feel comfortable memorizing your PINs and passwords and feel you must write them down. Be sure you store your lists in a locked, secure location. Don't let anyone else know where you keep the information, and don't lend the key to anyone. Also, store your PINs in a different location as your plastic cards. A thief who can't guess your PIN will end up getting locked out of the system. This will be a good warning sign for you, and it will protect your money! Also, if don't intend to use a credit or debit card, don't carry it with you. Not only will this protect it from being stolen, it'll help you stay within your personal budget!

6. Keep a photocopy of your wallet's contents in a safe, locked place

Make sure you have a record of the contents of your wallet or purse. That way, you can easily report to each company if and when your belongings are lost or stolen. In case of loss, immediately notify every company involved and ask them to freeze your account.

7. Be smart when you choose your passwords

Avoid using common passwords based on your birth date, an anniversary, your phone number, or your pet's name. Mix letters with numbers and symbols. Avoid using the same password for all your accounts, but be sure each of your accounts is password protected. Finally, change your passwords at least twice a year.

8. Get regular credit reports

Request your one-time-a-year free credit report. You have a right to it. And if you can afford the additional cost, it would be better to get regular updates throughout the year. Intervals of 3 to 6 months will help you keep close track on your accounts and allow you to catch suspicious activity sooner. Call the three major agencies to get your report:

Equifax: P.O. Box 740241 Atlanta, GA 30374-0241
For emergencies, call 1-800-525-6285

Experian: P.O. Box 2002 Allen TX 75013
For emergencies, call 1-888-EXPERIAN (397-3742)
Trans Union: P.O. Box 1000, Chester, PA 19022
For emergencies, call 1-800-680-7289

9. Review your bills when you receive them, and keep them in a locked safe place

Be sure to note all purchases and transactions on your monthly statements to be sure you are familiar with them. If you find a transaction you did not authorize, act on it immediately. Notify the company of your suspicions and submit a dispute with the vendor. Save your old statements for at least a year in case a problem arises. And keep your personal papers under lock and key. This would include birth certificates and social security cards; applications for mortgages, loans, and credit cards; and bills, invoices, and monthly statements. These documents are rich with personal information that will be a goldmine to an identity thief. If you can, keep these papers in a safe deposit box where only you and one other trusted person know the location and/or have a key.

10. Invest in a good paper shredder

The best way to protect personal information on papers you don't want to keep is to use a cross-cut paper shredder to destroy them before you throw them away. This should include outdated credit receipts, credit application copies, insurance forms you don't need anymore, physician invoices and reports, old checks and bank statements, and expired credit cards you don't intend to renew or use again. Do yourself a favor and immediately shred pre-approved credit applications.

11. Be careful with your credit cards

If at all possible, ask for a photo ID type credit card. And when you use it, note whether the clerk checks your signature against the one on the card. If they don't, you might want to avoid that store in the future. Don't let a waitress or waiter walk away with your credit card. Better to pay cash at restaurants than to risk the copy-it-while-I-have-it scam.

12. Use common sense online

Use encrypted or secure servers when you sign into financial accounts or make online purchases. Do not do business with websites you haven't heard of before. Don't open files sent to you by people you don't know. For that matter, don't open e-mails from strangers. Delete them immediately. Install and maintain current anti-virus, firewall, and adware software to block and delete malicious cookies and spyware before it does any damage. Set your browser to refuse to open pop-ups without your approval. Be careful and suspicious online. You can't see the person or people at the other end, and you don't know what their intentions are. Limit your online purchases to well-known businesses and places where you already have an account.

How To Avoid Becoming A Victim Of Identity Theft?

Simply put, identity theft happens when someone assumes another person's identity in order to fraudulently obtain money, goods, or services. The results of identity theft include ruined credit ratings, unearned debt, unwanted debt collections, and sometimes even wrongful arrest.

Identity theft is a malicious and onerous crime because most victims will not find out they're a victim until the damage is already done, because it costs the victim so much, and because offenders usually get away with the crime.

Reports of identity theft continue to increase at an alarming rate each year. As many as 10 million people fall victim to this crime annually. Victims report that the experience is as traumatic as being mugged or having their home burglarized. It's an invasion of your privacy and an attack on your personal financial well-being. It undermines your sense of trust in others and creates fear of becoming a victim again in the future.

Identity Theft – Don't Be The Next Victim!

What does Identity Theft Involve?

Identity theft happens when someone gets access to your personal information. This may be your birth date, your social security or driver's license number, your bank and credit account numbers, or your PINs or passwords. Having one piece of the information puzzle makes it easier to get others. For example, knowing your birth date may give the thief enough information to trick other information out of an unsuspecting office clerk.

Once the thief has your information, they can make purchases, open new accounts, or make loans under your name. It is common for identity thieves to submit a change of address to your financial network so that you don't even receive your statements, making it more difficult for you to discover the fraud.
They can run your bills to and above your credit limits. They can apply for mortgages and loans using your credit history. The can even transfer money out of your bank accounts. Unfortunately, you won't know about it until one of your valid purchases is refused by a merchant or you get a phone call or letter from a debt collector.

In the worst cases, identity thieves have committed other serious crimes under their victim's identity. Wrongful arrest and very expensive defense costs can result for the victim.

Technology is a Double-Edged Sword

One reason identity theft is on the rise is the increasing use of electronic media for making financial transactions. Shopping over the internet is common today, and many purchases are made over the telephone. Buyers and sellers don't come into contact. Signatures can't be verified long distance. Security issues abound on the internet, and it is fairly easy to get your information through non-secure websites.

Hackers develop sophisticated programs that steal information as you enter it or download entire customer databases from large companies, including the customers' personal information.

Many people fail to keep their account numbers, passwords, and PINs within their control. They write them down, carry the list of numbers with them (where they can be stolen), or leave them out where others can get the information. They use passwords that are easy to guess (birth dates, anniversaries, pet's names, etc.) rather than more complex combinations of numbers, letters, and symbols. They use the same password for all their accounts or fail to change their passwords from time to time.

Advice for Potential Victims of Identity Theft

The U.S. Department of Commerce's Federal Trade Commission (FTC) has published guidelines to help citizens avoid becoming victims of identity theft:

* Never give out more information than is necessary. Especially when shopping online or via telephone, limit your information to that necessary to make the purchase and receive the product or service. Don't volunteer anything you don't have to.

* If you suspect someone is trying to get information from you under false pretenses (like an e- mail asking you to verify account information), contact the company in question to ask them if they sent the e-mail and why they are asking for the information. Often, the company is a victim of fraudulent activities as well. If they do not acknowledge the e-mail as theirs, forward a copy of the e-mail to the ISP that delivered it and to the FTC. You can also send an alert to the major consumer reporting companies (Equifax, TransUnion, and Experian) so that they are aware of the abuse.

* If you can, have your entire bank and credit accounts and lines of credit password protected so that no one can make a transaction without proper authorization. Use smart passwords that are not easy to guess.

* Keep your social security and credit cards in a safe place under lock and key. Consider putting them with other important personal documents in a safe deposit box or home safe. Avoid carrying your account numbers in your wallet or purse, and don't share the information with co- workers and acquaintances. Don't keep anything in your wallet that you can't afford to lose.

* Don't give out your social security number unless you have to secure a credit report, open an account, or apply for a loan.

* Don't use websites that are not secured. Make purchases and provide personal information ONLY over secure servers. Look for URLs that use "https://" and encryption software to process information they gather from customers. Find out what their privacy policies are and whether they use the information you give them for any other purposes. Base your decision on whether to proceed on their answers to those questions.

Avoid Becoming Another Hopeless Victim Of Bank Identity Theft

Identity theft is in fact quite a complicated and impressive process.
These thieves are smart people who can go to great lengths and use technology to steal your identity. It can cause you monetary damage and stress, if not more. There have been incidents where the wrong individuals have faced court harassment thanks to the fact that an identity thief had committed a crime under their name!

In more cases than not, by the time you find out about such misuse of your identity, the criminal is well hidden under a different one. You are left with a bad reputation and a lot of paper work to take care of with the bank and maybe the police. Being the victim of such a crime is not easy to shake off. At first you have to prove yourself innocent of any crime that has been committed under your identity, and then you have to prove it over and over again to people through the years.

Did you know that bank identity theft is nothing new? It's been around for many years before we even had credit cards or electronic banking. It is the process of withdrawing funds from a person's account under the pretense of being that person. This could happen if the person who holds the account has not visited the bank for many years. The imposter could show up as the account holder, and sign a well forged signature to withdraw huge funds. In another kind of bank identity theft, the thief could pose as an individual with a good credit rating, if he or she had access to this person's personal details such as credit rating and social security number. Once they prove this they can take a huge loan and disappear, leaving the bank looking for the wrong guy!

Identity theft can occur thanks to any of your personal information falling into the wrong hands. A drivers' license, an email password or a credit card pin - any such information can give an identity thief an inlay into your life and identity. Here are a few warning signs that should alert you when someone is accessing your account -

1. You are billed for a credit card that you never did apply for in the first place. Report this to the bank and to the police immediately.

2. You see charges on your credit statement that you never authorized.

3. Your statements are unusually late.

4. *Your bank statements speak on transactions that are new to you.*

5. *Collection agents notify you regarding credit accounts you never opened.*

6. *Follow up calls from customer service departments - about consumables you did not purchase.*

7. *Debts displayed on the credit report - ones that you did not file for.*

When you see any of these signs, call the bank to verify your statement immediately.

Ways To Protect Yourself From Computer Identity Theft

A disposable Email ID

It is always safe to have an alternative email id than your business id. For instance, if you would like to use an email id to buy something online or to download a product, you could use the disposable one. This way, even if someone did crack this password they would not be able to get in touch with your business partners. You could use something like yahoo and maybe Hotmail for this purpose - here you can make any number of IDs for free you know.

Hide your identity

If you go by the name John Smith, it would be foolish to make an email id that read john.smith@ something. This is what hackers will target first, if someone is trying to fake your identity on the net. When choosing a password, don't use something as obvious as your date of birth - that is not personal enough for no one else to know. Instead you could use something like the name of your first pet, or the name of your favorite model car.

Unique Passwords

I know it is convenient to use the same password for all your card pins. Don't make the same mistake with your email ids. If you do this, when a hacker cracks one email id, he's cracked all of them. The answer is - don't use so many ids that you cannot remember the unique passwords, but do have an alternate id with a UNIQUE password.

Change of Password

Why not change your password every few months? That is a great idea to stay secure. More often than not, when a hacker gets into your mail id, he or she will wait a few weeks or months to see how they can take advantage of your information. You never know when someone reads your email right after you do. So, it is good to change your password every few months just in case someone's broken in and it's still not too late (meaning no damage has yet been done).

Don't Risk Many Cards Online

If you use a lot of cards, keep only one, maybe one with the lowest limit for your online usage. Why risk all of the cards by using them online? When you stick to only one card online, even when there is a security breach, you will only have one bank to deal with. Imagine trying to change all your credit cards overnight - not a very happy thought. And that is exactly what you will have to do if you use many cards online and security is breached on all of them.

Get Secure With Online Payment Methods

Websites like PayPal and money bookers are the answer to buying goods online. You only need to reveal your credit card details to them, and then make all your purchases through them.

Not Being One Of Those Listed In The History Of Identity Theft Crimes

Everything has changed in today's world thanks to the internet, and crime has seen a new face as well. No more guns - it only takes an internet connection for the smart thief of today to do his thing.

We usually see someone 'stealing' another person's identity on the internet, to be able to use his or her money. However at times it is done for the sake of deception. The only way it can be done is when the 'thief' finds out personal information such as your email password, your credit card pin number and your social security number.

Theft of Credit Card Information
This is the most common kind of identity theft on the internet, and the federal bureau has literally thousands of complaints of such fraudulent card usage every year. It's as simple as this - you use your credit card on a web site to buy a bouquet for your baby back home. The website is a fraudulent one. Not only do they not deliver the goods, they use your personal information for their own benefit.

More often than not such companies are not even companies, but individuals posing as organizations simply to get your personal information in their hands. At times, the company could be genuine but not the employee who has access to your information. Yet another possibility is a hacker getting into the company's database through the internet and stealing all their secure information. And that includes their customers' secure information as well!
The more dangerous kind of identity theft

If someone got hold of your social security number, date of birth and such details - did you know they could operate bank accounts, email ids and credit cards in your name?

At first thought you may think it cannot really harm you unless they actually take your money and use it. Wrong! Terrorists try and get hold of such information to operate under seemingly innocent identities for the transfer of money from one account to another. By the time something does look fishy and the feds show up - they are already gone, and you have a lot of answering to possibly do!

Yes technology has advanced a great deal today, and like every other kind, the internet technology is a power with which must come responsibility.

Imagine someone who opens a bank account using your id. They then are sent a credit card in your name. They are sent the PIN as well! They use the card; you are totally unaware until the bill for a completely unknown card arrives in your mail box. This is the classic case of identity theft.

Try and keep yourself up to date with information on the current threats to identity, and that is the only way you can stay secure against identity thieves.

Nine Ways To Prevent Identity Theft

What Identity Theft is

Maybe you have heard many recent news stories concerning identity thefts. It is basically the use of your personal social security number, driver's license number or maybe even something like your mother's maiden name (many internet sites ask for that), by an unauthorized person, meaning someone other than your own self. That is not a very comforting thought, i am sure you will agree. It is good to stay prepared for the event that such misfortune may befall you. It does sound like too much at first. But imagine you go shopping, select your favorite trousers and when it is time to pay you are told your credit balance is next to zero on your card.

Only you know that it cannot be so - now you would need to follow up with the bank etc. Here is how you can take measures to prevent identity theft

At the house

1. If you are the kind who likes to take some of your work home, be careful not to let your personal data files get mixed up with work files on your hard drive.

2. As far as snail mail post goes, it is wiser to drop it off at the post office yourself rather than to leave it unattended in the mail box. Also, if you suddenly decide to go on a trip, do call the post office and ask them to hold your letters until you contact them again.

3. Do not throw away used bills, credit card statements and other personal finance data. Throwing them in the bin would allow someone to get at that information, if they have already targeted you. Instead, it is better to destroy such papers. use a shredder!

4. Do not keep all your eggs in one bank basket! Allot different accounts to your social security, insurance policies and credit cards.

And at the work place

5. Get to learn about the safety of data at the office. Someone always does have access to all your data and it is probably the network administrator.

6. Many of us use the internet to make finance transactions today. If you have clients online that are rated badly by other users, try and find out why. Never give out personal information to anyone over the internet, unless it is a trusted company.

7. Use something like a Pay Pal account to make online purchases. Every time you use your credit card you are increasing the risk of identity theft.

8. Never give your social security number, card pin or other personal information to an unknown tele caller. On the other hand, if you have made the call for a reason, it may be ok to do so.

9. Whenever you deal with a web site, look for their security policy.

Follow these steps and chances are your identity will remain yours!

9 Steps To Prevent Commercial Identity Theft

Has this ever happened in your life - you are in the best of moods and the phone rings. You answer it cheerfully only to be welcomed by a crude voice on the other end that says your bills are overdue. And after you have planned and paid out every single bill well in time? Well that kind of confusion is often caused by commercial identity theft. this can only happen when someone has already used your social security number, your credit card PIN, your drivers' license or your bank account. In other words it is more than just money at stake here - the thief has taken on your identity!

It is sad but true, that this HAS in fact happened to many people in recent times. To say they were upset with the situation would be an understatement. People do work hard to get what they do get in life, and then somebody can just take it away like that? It does not sound fair, and it sure is not.

To protect yourself and your family from such thieves, we've put down a few tips for you -

Identity Theft – Don't Be The Next Victim!

1. Do make checks on your credit report by the three firms more than just once in a year. Go through every little detail to verify its accuracy. Any smallest error needs to be immediately verified.

2. It is a bad idea to carry your social security number around in your wallet. Try and memorize it for emergency. If you lose your wallet, you should only lose the cash in it not your identity.

3. A classic mistake is when people write down their PIN numbers on the reverse of their ATM cards. What more could a thief ask for? Keep all private numbers including drivers' license number, social security and PIN, private.

4. The internet is the target for many hackers, and most people give out personal credit card information on the net while making a purchase. Don't do that. Use something like Pay Pal instead.

5. Do not let out your credit card private details to anybody who calls, especially to buy a product. That is not the right way to buy a product.

6. When spending time in a hotel room, do use the hotel phone rather than a mobile. Identity thieves love to listen on private conversations in hotel rooms and lobbies.

7. You could work with a company that prevents identity theft and helps with the paperwork if it does happen to you.

8. If you find a credit card, never do anything other than report it to the nearest authority. You could get involved with a scamming chain simply by carrying it around.

9. If you would like to speak to somebody about identity theft call the federal trade commission at 1-877-IDTHEFT (438-4338)

22 Tips For Identity Theft Prevention

1. Where this kind of a thief is concerned, he would rather steal things like your social security number than your cash. Because he can use it to get right into your commercial activities. So never write your social security number on your papers, in your wallet and in your mobile phone.

2. Have you heard about shoulder surfing? Its literally peeping over your shoulder to get your

ATM pin or similar details. Beware of prying eyes and hidden cameras.

3. Shred your important papers before you dispose of them.

4. Rather than put your signature on the credit cards, you could simply write down something like 'photo id available'. This prevents people using your card if they get their hands on it, at least at times.

5. When you are done with your digital files such as old budgets, bank statements and tax returns, delete the files rather than leave them on your computer at home or office.

6. Look carefully at all your bills and credit card statements - there may be a small amount being deducted to an internet site that you did not sign up for!

7. Rather than leave your bills in the post box, why not take a trip to the post office and pay them directly?

8. Give out limited details in writing, on cheques.

9. At least once a year, analyze all your credit reports. They have your social security number, your card numbers and other valuable info.

10. Make sure you have a good anti-virus and anti-spy ware installed on your PC.

11. Check that the website is secure before you pay for an item online.

12. Keep constant track on your credit.

13. If anyone asks you for personal information that seems unrelated to the task at hand, go ahead and ask why they want to know those details.

14. If you are being offered a pre - approved credit card that sounds fishy. Think again before you give in your personal details. The card may be a dummy, and your information would be real!

15. Do not carry valuable papers unless you need to use them.

16. Keep track of your yearly social security reports so you can pin point if anything is amiss.

17. Take note of every charge credited to your card before you pay the amount.

18. If you have a credit card account that you do not use, it is better to cancel it.

19. Never give your credit card number to a tele-caller. If you called THEM it is ok to do so at times.

20. It is wise to use a credit card monitoring service so you know as soon as someone applies in your name!

21. Verify a stranger's identity before you respond to their emails.

22. Keep your wallet protected in crowded places.

Learn How to Prevent Identity Theft

Nobody likes being victimized, and identity theft is becoming a recurring nuisance in the world today. Once the deed is done it is quite hard to reverse it, and a lot of paper work will be the least that you will need to do. It is surely much better to work at the prevention rather than the cure.

The one important point you need to always bear in mind is that if the thief cannot get at your personal information, he cannot steal your identity. Here is how they can get your personal valuable and sensitive information -

1. When you buy consumables over the internet

2. With web banks

3. Not destroying your old credit cards

4. Storage of critical information on a PC

5. Mobile phones

6. Wireless phones

These are the classic target areas the thieves are looking at and these are the areas you will need to safe guard. Here is a list of steps you may take to prevent identity theft -

1. Memorize your pin numbers and passwords rather than putting them down on paper.

2. Protect your critical computer files by locking them with a password, and do not use something as obvious as a birthday or the name or your girlfriend as the password!

3. Ask the credit bureau to give you regular updates on your credit, and look for anything out of the ordinary in the reports.

4. Use a good anti-virus and anti-spy ware on your PC. Here is where they most often get your passwords!

5. Where sensitive information is concerned, never email it. Give it personally over the phone if you must, or better still - in person at the next meeting.

6. When someone unknown sends you an email attachment, never download it without running a virus check on it - it is most probably a virus or a bug.

7. Never give your personal credit card pin number or security code to someone who calls you over the phone.

8. Destroy your used credit cards before you throw them away.

9. If you do happen to misplace or lose a credit card, drivers' license or any other personal information carrier, report it to the police, and also to your banks.

10. If you need to throw away documents containing your personal data, destroy them first. Use a shredder, or you could just burn them so they can never fall into wrong hands.

11. That goes for bank receipts and all your bills as well - destroy them rather than just throw them into the bin.

Following these few tips can save you a lot of trouble where identity theft is concerned. Remember the golden rule - prevention is better than cure. Keep your personal information secure, and your identity is secure.

12 Steps To Avoid Identity Theft With Your Stolen Checks

One of the easiest ways a fraudulent person can access your bank is through a check. All they need to do is pick your pocket, handbag or briefcase, and they might even get the whole check book filled with blank pages. Can you imagine what damage this person could do if he or she could forge your signature? If you do realize one day that your check is missing, it could very well be stolen by such a thief. Stop payments on all issued checks immediately, because you may not have issued them! Do get your bank statements, and speak with the bank officials to see if any of the leaves have already been used. In most cases it would be easier to verify this if you could provide the check numbers. If you are a regular check user and are aware and fearful of identity theft, you could use these measures to feel safer about the issue -

1. You could ask for a credit report from a credit agency to see if there are unusual transactions from your account. It may be a small transaction at first, as a 'trial run' to suck your money out little by little.

2. Write down all the check numbers every time you issue one - this way you would realize immediately when one or more leaves is missing and then go ahead and stop payment on them.

3. Don't keep all your eggs in one basket! Carry your passport, check books and other important personal papers in different bags/wallets.

4. Do not place any check account statement in your mailing box. that makes it an easy target for identity thieves.

5. Do ask for privacy procedure processes at the bank.

6. Keep all the check statements on record for future reference.

7. If you need a new check book, collect it personally at the bank rather than have it mailed to you. All a thief would need to do is break open your mail box!

8. It is a bad idea to write down your social security number on any check. This way, if you lose your check, you also just give your social security details to the thief.

9. take the time to review your bank statements as they are coming in. Look for any unusual transaction, and contact the bank to verify.

10. If you apply for a check account, ask for the return of application once it is approved - so it does not fall into the wrong hands.

11. Use all the space in the allotted area when writing out a check. Do not leave space for someone to add to it. Also, use a permanent marker when writing checks.

12. If you find a check missing from your book, call the police and call the bank before that.

Nine Ways To Combat Identity Theft

If a person wants your identity, nothing will prevent them from making you become a victim of identity theft.

What makes this crime so easy?

They can commit these crimes so easily because all too often, people mishandle important papers or are careless with information in the workplace. There are also too lenient credit industry practices and the total effortlessness of getting social security numbers.

You can reduce your chance of being the victim of fraud by following nine simple steps. These are:

- Regarding Credit and Debit Reports

1. Do not let it become habit on carrying both the credit and debit cards at the same time. It's also a wise idea not to use the debit card because they lose more out of the checking account.

However, you can carry at least one credit card on you, perhaps two as well as your ATM card.
Should you be used to the debit card, regularly check your online account to detect signs of fraud or theft. As soon as you see discrepancies, report it to your bank or Credit Card Company.

2. When using the debit or credit card, be cautious about how these cards are swiped and how they are handled.

Some restaurant employees and many other places are using non-detectable skimmers that can pull off account numbers from personal computers. By getting this information, they can achieve to buy products online or make counterfeit cards.

3. Never use your debit card online when you shop. Instead use a credit card. These cards often offer better protection in case of fraud.

4. Keep a list of the cards you have and make a separate list for account numbers, expiration dates and customer service phone numbers in case the cards are lost or stolen.

Put these in a safe place so you can use them for immediate access should you need to.

5. Never give out your personal information out online, by phone or by mail. Only if you trust the person enough do you attempt to do this.

A strategy thieves like to use is calling victims by saying they have won a prize of some sort but the only way to get the money is to give out personal data. Never do this!

6. Don't throw your receipts just anywhere. Shred them if they are not needed and place them in a trash can not frequently used.

Place shopping receipts inside your purse or wallet, not on your bag.

7. Never write your credit card number on your checks. This is a violation in some states but really exposes it to thieves.

Doing this opens you up to being a victim.

8. Check the mailbox especially if you are waiting on something important including credit cards or credit statements. People could be peeking out to steal them before you can check.

Should the card not arrive when it is supposed to call the credit company to be sure the card did not fall into the wrong hands.

9. Do not forget to request your credit report once a year. A law was passed so the three credit bureaus have to give you a free copy each year.

Should your report show signs of mishandling or unusual charges or credit reporting, look into them and make disputes.

The sooner the fraud is found, the quicker it can be resolved and get your finances back in order.

It is so important to remember these tips because it can make the difference between having good credit and having negative aspects by credit issuers who think you are the one making
bad marks.

ID Theft Protection - How You Can Protect Yourself

Have you ever gotten a credit card bill you know is not yours or do you have a credit card that has large purchase amounts that you did not buy?

What about a criminal record? Where you pulled over for outstanding tickets or warrants but you've never been in trouble with the law before?

Then you've more than likely been an identity theft victim. This can be a heartbreaking task to clear up.

Identity theft is a very frustrating and damaging crime for those who have been targeted by criminals. The thieves can steal your hard earned cash as well as ruin your reputation.

What else can these criminals do?

Some of the things these criminals can do is ruin you both financial, economically and criminally. Here are some things they try for:

- Financial fraud

- Bank account fraud

- Computer fraud

- Criminal activities using your name

Imagine if you will be investigated for crimes you have no idea about. Something has simple as stealing lipstick or food and they can use your name as theirs.

This is so upsetting for both the person whose name is being used and the family of the person whose name is used. Criminal activity is not easy to fix once your name is in the computer system.

These criminals will get you convicted for tax evasion and fraud if you are not protecting your information and looking over it continuously. How can thieves get this information? Thieves can get your data in a variety of ways. It can be as simple as clicking on a computer e-mail that has a link in it or losing your credit card outside your home.

Everyone should know how to protect themselves from these technologically advanced predators. Always be careful to whom you give out your personal information to.

Listed below are eight ways a person can protect themselves from being a victim of identity theft
(These are not listed in the order of importance.):

- Should the phone ring and a person identifies themselves with a company you do business with, asking to verify some information.

Do NOT give this to them! Get a name, full one preferably, and hang up on them. Call the company back... asking if they did indeed call.

- Should you ever give out your personal information to a company, be sure it is with one that is reputable, one that will protect your information. Ask them how they will protect your data.

- Always keep track of credit card receipts and credit card statements. Keep a constant eye on your bank statements too. Thieves who want to use your good name all the time will buy only one item a statement period to throw off suspicion of anything being out of place.

- Shred, rip up or cut up any personal information or papers. Thieves do not mind going dumpster diving for personal data.

- Never carry documents you do not need in your purse or wallet. A simple crime in stealing these items can turn into a devastating nightmare of identity theft.

- Make copies of credit cards, passports and other sensitive data. Doing so will make it easier to cancel if they are compromised.

- Keep up with your deposit slips. These are the easiest way a thief can get your bank account number. Keep it safe in your home at all times.

- Use a secure password, not one that can be easily guessed such as your birthday or mother's maiden name.

Contact police if you feel you've been a victim of identity theft. From here, you can get unauthorized marks off your credit report easier.

Steps To Prevent Identity Theft

Identity theft… this is a most serious crime plaguing people today. If you have been the prey of this, you know it can have serious repercussions. It can be very troublesome clearing your credit, getting into debt, losing money and even possible to get into trouble with the law. It could be difficult in obtaining a job or a place to live. Landlords do check applicants' credit reports.

Thieves need your credit card numbers, name, address, social security number and other personal data to hijack your identity. Once the thieves do this, they can open bank accounts, make purchases, apply for loans, try for new credit cards, get government benefits and forge checks with your name on it.

Should you be a victim, contact the authorities immediately. From here, you can apply for identity theft insurance. The option is available on some homeowner's policy. Having the insurance doesn't guarantee that no one won't still your identity; it only helps you recover should you be a victim.

Be careful with your personal data, as this is the best prevention. You won't know until afterwards that someone has stolen it.

Listed below are six ways thieves can get your identity:

Steal your wallet that contains your credit cards and other information; Go through trashcans for personal data;

Providing personal information through e-mail or registration based websites; Pretending to be a new creditor, offering you credit;

Eaves dropping on conversations or looking over your shoulder as you use your information; Pretend to promise awards or prizes by e-mail.

There are four transactions that can cause worry. They are:

Online banking; Online purchases;
Storing personal information on computer;

Using social security information for ID purposes.

It does not mean you should ignore these types of transactions just be careful when you do and do not give out your personal information.

However, this does not necessarily mean that you should avoid these transactions. It means that you should be careful when giving away your personal and financial information. Be aware of how your use it and your financial information to stop identity theft altogether.

There are 11 tips to follow to safeguard your information... personal and financial.

- Remember your social security number.

- Remember your PIN numbers.

- For passwords, use something hard not a birthday or a maiden name.

- Protect your computer against Spywares by installing and updating firewall software.

- Confirm a website's legitimacy when it asks for personal data.

- Beware of e-mails with attachments from some you do not know or asks you to click on links

- When websites are asking for personal data they should be secured. Two ways this happens is the "S" in https and the lock on the websites next to the address bar.

- Do not give out personal information over the phone unless you made the initial contact.

- Should you lost or misplaced your credit cards, contact the company and cancel them.

- Easier said than done but pick your mail up as soon as it is delivered.

- Don't get rid of financial and personal data in public areas.

By safeguarding this information, it will make it harder for thieves to obtain your identity. Know what you are throwing away and practice these eleven rules.

Always remember to shred, cut up or puncture any documents that contain any of the personal data. That includes all credit cards, used checks and identity cards. They could eventually get into the wrong hands.

Should you think something is amiss, report it at once, getting it in black and white.

Identity Theft Protection: What Not to Do

To be a smart consumer, identity theft protection is something that should always be top of your mind. You should know what you should do and what you should not do in order to insure that you do not become a victim. There are several things that you should do, or rather things that you should not do to make sure that this does not happen to you.

Identity Theft – Don't Be The Next Victim!

The statistics show that many people will have some form of mistake on their credit report that has to do with identity theft. Here are some things that you should know about now. These are your do not do's.

- *Never provide your social security number to anyone. You should always safely guard this information. In some states, you do not have to have it on your driver's license either.*

- *When you are careful about using your social security number, those that may be able to apply for and get credit in your name will have that much of a more difficult time doing so.*

- *Don't wait if it's lost. If you lose your credit card, do not wait to cancel it. If you can't find it, then take the time to look for it now. If you cannot find it, call the credit card company immediately and have them cancel and reissue it. Most credit card use on your credit card will be done within the first 24 hours of the thief having it in their possession.*

- *Don't give out your address, bank account information or your last name. In some cases, this may be enough to get moving on a loan. Those that know that you have a good credit history may target you for this type of information. This information should not be given out on the web either.*

- *Don't forget about spyware and online protection. You should always have your online spyware running. This can help you to keep those that are using spyware as an identity theft tool to not attack you. Also, make sure you only provide your credit information on the web through merchants you know and those that offer a secure website.*

- *Don't go with the wrong credit card company. Most will offer identity theft protection in case someone does get a hold of your information. Choose your credit card company only after considering what they offer in identity theft protection.*

These things are all things that you should do, all the time, to insure that you do not become a victim here.

Credit Cards and Identity Theft Protection

If you use credit cards, there are several things that you should do now, to make sure that you are covered if someone should try to pull a case of identity theft on you. Credit cards are often the single simplest method for those that are looking to steal to do so. To do this, they simply need to gather some information from you and then off they can go to make the purchases that they would like to on your dime. But, many credit cards now offer identity theft protection. This is a way of protecting you from the theft of your money on your credit card.

Each credit card company does offer something that is different. You should take the necessary steps, then to insure that the credit cards that you choose to work with will provide you with the best quality of protection. You should always consider this type of protection as it can work just like an insurance policy to protect you when and if something goes wrong. Find out before you sign up with a company what type of protection they offer.

What Is It?

What is this type of identity theft protection? While each credit card company is different, most will offer you the same basic things. For example, if you call to report that your credit card is missing or stolen, they will freeze the account which means that no one, even you, can use it until it is deemed that all is well. They can then go back and make sure that no one has used your account in the time period that the credit card was missing. If they have, the protection will kick in.

Most of the credit cards out there will offer you some sort of protection. Most will do this through not holding you responsible for debts that you have not incurred.

You will need to show that the transactions that were purchased on your credit card were in fact not made by you. If you go to use your credit card and you know that you do have available credit, but your credit card has somehow been denied, this may be a sign that there is identity theft. You should immediately call your credit card lender and inquire as to what has happened on your account. Most lenders will help you to sort through the problems and will get your available balance back to you quickly.

Identity theft protection is necessary for anyone that uses credit cards. Learn what your bank or lending company offers so that you are always protected.

Identity Theft Using Credit Card

You had a great weekend. You and your best friend went shopping the mall. At the mall, you picked up some cash at the ATM and you some great bargains at a couple of sales. Afterward, you went out for dinner and drinks to discuss the week's events and gossip about the rest of the crowd. After dinner, you gave your credit card to the waitress, signed the bill, and went home for a good night's sleep.

On Monday, life gets back to normal, and the job beckons. But this Monday is different. With today's mail is your credit card billing statement. Relaxing from work, you review the statement. What's this? There are purchases on the statement for things you know you didn't buy. And the balance is through the roof! What is going on?

You call the credit card company to find out what's happened. They are helpful but not very sympathetic. They note you're near your credit limit and suggest you may a hefty payment this month. They don't understand. You did NOT make those purchases. What can you do now?

If you've been through this before, you know you've been a victim of a crime. Call it identity theft or credit card fraud, it's illegal, and it carries penalties IF the criminal gets caught. Somehow, someone has gotten hold of your personal financial information. They've used your credit and your credit record to steal from both you and the credit card company. The problem is, now the credit card company wants you to pay the bill. If you don't, it will hurt your credit score and make it more difficult to get loans at a good rate or open a new account in the future. You're in a jam, and the criminal who stole your identity is out partying on your good credit.

How could this have happened? Was there someone standing behind you at the ATM, observing you enter your PIN for cash? Or did the waitress leave your card unattended out on a counter at the restaurant? Did you forget your card at the restaurant? Better check your wallet to be sure. You feel violated, as if someone had broken into your home. And this criminal doesn't have a face or a name. You have no idea who or where the identity theft is. And you don't have a clue about what to do about it.

Criminals like this commit identity theft by getting access to your personal information. They can use your birth date, your social security or driver's license number, your account numbers, your

PINs and your passwords to sneak into your accounts and rob you. In 2003, around 10 million people were victims of identity theft, and it cost them a total of $5 billion out-of-pocket. It also cost merchants and financial institutions $50 billion in that year. Each victim of identity theft ended up spending from $500 to $1200 and from 30 to 60 hours of personal time trying to resolve the problem. And these thefts took place over a three- to six-month period.

How can they get away with this malicious crime? It's an increasing problem due to our wonderful technology and the internet.

Often, buyers and sellers don't have personal face-to- face contact. Transactions take place over the internet or telephone. The seller doesn't see the identity thief and can't identify them.

All the criminal has to do is give them a different shipping address from your billing address. Some identity thieves even submit change of address information to your bank and credit accounts, making it more difficult for you to spot unauthorized transactions.

Why don't people find out about identity theft sooner? You may be surprised, but most people don't check their statements as soon as they get them. They may set them aside, making payments on the balance without reviewing the purchases and giving the thief even more time to run up a big tab.

Even when the theft is discovered, it's very difficult to find the perpetrator. They're using your address and information. Bogus shipping addresses may go to a post office box or postal service. They may even go to a non-existent address. All the thief has to do is monitor for deliveries.

Another reason it's hard to prevent identity theft on your credit cards is that no one knows about it until the monthly billing statement goes out. As mentioned before, only the most diligent credit card holders catch these abuses quickly when they review their statements. Some people assume the credit card company's records are accurate.

They may even assume they made the purchase when, in fact, it was an identity thief. Normally, identity thieves who prey upon credit cards make as many purchases as they can in the days immediately following the theft. They can quickly reach your credit limit and often exceed it. You find out about it when your purchases are refused by the company or when the debt collector calls.

Identity Theft – Don't Be The Next Victim!

Having a little of your personal information gives access to the rest of your information. Identity thieves often misrepresent themselves, calling your bank or credit card company with a piece of personal information to learn more about your accounts. When this happens, you become even more vulnerable.

Pretending to be you, they can transfer money out of your accounts, change your address, and apply for mortgages or loans. They may even rent apartments or apply for jobs, masquerading as you.

If you think you've become a victim of identity theft, you should immediately take action to stop the crime or maybe even catch the thief:

- Immediately file a police report. Do not pass go. Do not wait a day or two. As soon as you're aware of fraudulent purchases or misrepresentations, contact your local police. You can also call the local U.S. Attorney's Office. Identity theft is often considered a federal crime, depending on the circumstances. When you've made your report, be sure to get and keep a copy of it so that you can provide the information to your bank and creditors.

- File a report with the postal service. This may help you find out where goods were delivered and prevent the continued use of a bogus address.

- Notify the credit bureau. Immediately inform at least one of the three major credit reporting agencies (Equifax, TransUnion, or Experian). You may qualify for a free credit report. You can also freeze your credit reporting. That way, you will be alerted if anyone makes a credit inquiry or tries to open a new account in your name. There is a small fee for freezing the report, but its well worth it to protect further abuses.

- Notify your bank and all your creditors of the crime. Close your accounts and reopen them so that you change all your account numbers.

If they'll agree to do it, assign a special password to your account so that transactions can't be processed without your express authorization. And make sure that check verification companies are aware of the problem so that they will not authorize the use of fake or stolen checks.

- Change your PINs and passwords immediately. If you must keep a written list of them, keep that list under lock and key, and don't share it with anyone. If you keep them in an electronic file, be sure to password protect the file. When you change your passwords, use new ones that combine letters, numbers, and symbols. And for heaven's sake, don't use the standard birth date, anniversary, or pet's name. Think of something unusual, something people who know you won't likely guess.

Identity theft is a serious, and increasing, crime. No one is immune. If you become a victim of this callous crime, you should act immediately to stop the activity and to help law enforcement catch and prosecute the perpetrator. Be sure that every company with which you have financial dealings is aware of the problem. Alert them quickly and get their cooperation in stopping and catching the thief.

We've all heard the nightmare stories from victims of identity theft. Tales of expenses and time lost to repairing good credit abound. In the most extreme cases, identity thieves commit other crimes using their victim's personal information, so you can even get in trouble with the law as a victim of identity theft.

Be vigilant. Be suspicious when it comes to your financial information and accounts. Guard your information carefully. Review financial documents as soon as you receive them, and follow up immediately if you find problems.

You may not be able to control every aspect of your financial record, but you can take many common-sense steps to protect it and prevent identity theft from making you the next victim.

Credit Reports and Identity Theft Protection

Believe it or not, one of the best ways to prevent identity theft from ruining your life is to make sure that you have an idea of what is happening with your credit. While you may think that the only thing that you can do is to make sure that your credit card balances are okay and make sure that no one is charging anything extra to your account. But, there is much more that you can do in the way of identity theft protection. One of those ways has a lot to do with your credit reporting agencies.

A credit reporting agency tracks the accounts that you have your balances on them and even figures out for other lenders if you are a good risk or if you are a really bad one. Whenever you go to open a new account, the credit grantors will look at what the credit reporting agencies have on you and make their decision based on that. If you have poor credit ratings listed there, you may actually be getting the interest rates or the loans that you want and that you deserve.

For most people, this is because they have mismanaged money or have quite a bit of credit as it is.

Yet, it may be because someone that got a hold of your personal information is now using it against you. If someone opens a credit card account using your social security number, you are going to run into a problem. But, it will likely come up on your credit report that you have this additional account. For that reason, you need to make sure that you know what is on your credit report, on a regular basis, so that you can insure that what your credit grantors see is really what you have earned.

To do this, you should at least monitor your credit report on a yearly basis. In the United States, law has been put into practice that says that the credit reporting agencies are required to provide you with a free credit report of yours each year. There is no reason, then, that you should not have a report in your hand to check for identity theft. You should take a close look at the information listed there. Look for this.

- Is there an account that you do not have? This may be something that is new or old.

- Is there a false address listed on your report? If someone tried to open an account with your social security number with a different address, this is going to show up here.

- Are there any other mistakes on your credit report including inquiries into it that you may not have made or allowed to be made?

Identity theft protection comes only when you know what to do to protect yourself. You should know what is being reported about you on your credit report..

If you haven't looked at yours lately, now is the ideal time to do so.

What Can I Do To Protect My Personal Credit?

It's not easy to protect yourself from identity theft. Most of it is intended to occur without your knowledge or consent. And there are many avenues for identity theft that are outside your control. But there are some things you can do to lessen the chances for identity theft.

- Secure your personal information at all times. Don't leave lists of account numbers unlocked, and don't share your user IDs or passwords with ANYone. Maintain as much control over your personal financial information as you can.

- Don't throw mail away if in contains any personal information, including your full name and address. Shred these documents before putting them in the garbage.

- Educate yourself about the techniques and tactics used in identity theft and protect yourself accordingly.

- Don't share personal account information with anyone, including co-workers, friends, and roommates. Unless they are also responsible for paying your bills, they have no reason to have this information. And don't give them your passwords without a very good reason. If you do share your passwords, change them as soon as possible.

- Shred unwanted and pre-approved credit applications, and have your name removed from those mailing lists.

- Be careful when you make purchases online to use only secure servers and to carefully guard your information. Do not keep a written list of passwords, and use passwords that are difficult to figure out (rather than something simple like your phone number).

How Do I know if Someone is Using my Personal Information?

Many victims of identity theft are not aware of the problem until they are refused credit or receive a bill for purchases they did not make. There are a few ways to catch identity theft early on:

- *Request your credit report from one or all of the three major credit reporting companies (Experian, TransUnion, and Equifax). Review the reports carefully to assure you are aware of and agree with the status on all accounts. Make sure there are no accounts you don't know about listed there. And check all recent credit inquiries. Companies from which you have not asked for an account should not be making inquiries. This is a sure sign that someone is out there using your name and information.*

- *When you review your credit report, immediately contact the reporting company and your creditor about any errors. Make sure individual account information is accurate and up-to-date, and be very persistent in getting errors corrected.*
You may have to provide documentation for corrections, and you will most likely have to contact the companies several times before the corrections show up in your report.

- *Review your account statements immediately when your receive them. Be sure you are aware and approve of all transactions. Check to be sure recent payments are reflected. Make sure they have the correct address. If you find errors on bank or credit card statements, contact the company immediately and continue to communicate with them until the corrections are reflected in your statements.*

What if I Am Already a Victim of Identity Theft?

If you think someone else is using your identity or personal financial information inappropriately, contact the nearest office of the U.S. Department of Justice. Contact your creditors to alert them to the fraud. Also inform your bank of the activity and secure their agreement to help protect your information. You may want to revisit the names of people authorized to access your personal financial information and limit it to essential parties only.

Find out as much as you can about the accounts, purchases, and applications the identity thief has made using your name. Then contact those companies directly and immediately to make sure they close the accounts and notify law enforcement when they become aware of any additional transactions.

3 Ways To Protect Yourself, Your Reputation And Your Credit

No doubt that identity theft is a national problem. There are things as an average citizen you need to know. Remember that everyone of any age including babies and children can be a victim of identity theft so educating yourself should be top priority in spotting identity theft.

You may be asking yourself how you can do this. By following these three important rules:

- **Identify the identity theft**

Most victims are not aware they have been preyed upon until notices of unpaid bills are charges on credit card bills are due. This can put a huge weight on their shoulder, affecting them mentally, emotionally and physically.

Some may say you are going overboard by doubling or even tripling your precautions. This is even more important for people whose credit history is impeccable. Thieves always look for these people first. These thieves are smart because they know if a person's credit is good, they can do extreme amounts of damage.

Once the thieves have control of your marked credit, they can open new credit accounts plus use your personal data to place counterfeit checks out, transfer money out of your bank account and obtain a job.

Should you be applying a loan to buy a house and you are denied, this should send a warning flag. Also, calls and letters will be coming in for things you were approved for or denied for on things you know you never applied for. Plus there will be purchases on existing credit card holdings or a utility bill at different addresses.

Be immediately suspicious if you notice you aren't getting the bank or credit statements or anything else you would get on a regular basis.

- Take countermeasures

To avoid being one of the victims, remember what actions you need to take to prevent it.

Do not give out personal data to just anyone. Never give it out over the phone or Internet. Check statements regularly. These crimes happen because people take for granted their security and do not check their credit card or bank statements on a regular basis. Keep on hand past statements to compare with the current one.

You don't need to take all your papers with you everywhere you go. Carrying a passport or social security card in your wallet or purse can be dangerous. Do not throw receipts just anywhere either.

Make sure your mailbox is secured. Get the mail once it has arrived if possible and if you plan to leave, get someone your trust to get your mail for you.
Shred anything that has personal information on you in it especially if you plan to throw these items away. Make sure the information cannot be visible once it's been rid of.

- Don't be afraid to ask for help

When surveyed, 60 percent of victims said they did not report the theft to police. Do call the police if you know you have been a victim. Request a copy of the credit report from the three bureaus and dispute what you feel is fraudulent.

If your credit cards are stolen, make sure to let the company know this. This goes for bank checks as well. Close accounts and open new ones. If you had a debit card, cancel it and use another password.

Should you be one of the few who get a new social security number, be careful when establishing new credit under it? It might get confusing when you are trying to repair the first one.

Following the above guidelines ensures your credit report is a safe as you can make it.

Identity Theft Protection: Using Your Credit Report

One of the things that you can do when it comes to identity theft protection is to use your credit report to help you. There are several ways that this can help you but the bottom line is that you need to do it.

Your credit report is a detailed report that is offered by several companies. It helps you and credit lenders to see just how much of a risk you are based on your past history of credit as well as your current amount of credit. By taking a good look at these things that the reporting agency is providing, the lender will make decisions such as if they will lend you money to buy a car or a home and if they will extend any other form of credit to you.

But, if you are a victim of identity theft, you may find yourself in a whole world of trouble. Your credit report is a good way to see if someone is actually using your information against you.

To know this, you should take the time to find out what is on your report. Each individual that has one is entitled to receive a free credit report each year from the credit reporting agencies in the US. This can be done right on the web making it much faster for you to handle problems as well.

You should check for several things on your credit report. First, you should insure that there are no new accounts (or old ones) on your credit report that you did not open and use. If you did not open the account and it has a balance on it, chances are that someone else did. Look at the inquires that are listed on your credit report as well. This will help you to see just who is looking at your report. Finally, make sure that the addresses that are listed there are really yours.

Check Credit Report Regularly And Beware Of Identity Theft

If you've ever made a major purchase like a home or automobile, you should know how important credit reports are to your life. Credit reports are used for much more than just checking your ability to pay a debt. Many service companies (apartments, auto insurance, cable TV, etc.) check your credit reports before they approve your application. Potential employers are likely to check your credit reports before they make the decision to hire you. Credit reports are the single most valuable tool for you to find out if you've become the victim of identity theft.

Your credit report score is a number ranging from 330 to 830, calculated based on a complex and high-protected algorithm. The higher your credit score, the better your credit. A good credit report score makes it more likely that your loan or credit application will be approved, and it makes it more likely that you'll get a favorable interest rate on money borrowed (whether through a loan or credit card).

Three companies (Experian, TransUnion, and Equifax) are the major credit report bureaus that collect and maintain information on your borrowing and repayment history, and they provide reports to your potential creditors upon request. U.S. citizens can by law request one free credit report each year, and you can sign up for a fee to maintain more regular access to your credit reports at all three companies.

What Information Do Credit Reports Contain?

Credit reports contain very detailed information about you including your legal name and any aliases you may have used, current and past addresses, employment history, and date of birth. They also contain details on your credit status that includes:

- *Current and past payment status (for example, number of payments over 30, 60, 90 days) on individual loans and credit accounts*

- *Total number of open and closed accounts, including the credit limit and account balance*

- *Whether payments on our accounts are current or delinquent*

- *Public record information like bankruptcy, local court records, liens, judgments, and child support records (This information that can stay in your record for up to 10 years.)*

- *Specific credit inquires made when we applied for loans or credit accounts in the past (kept very current)*

- *Detailed account history for each account (kept very current) indicating both on-time and overdue payments*

- *Credit card debt limit, account balance, and payment history (for active, open, AND closed accounts)*

- *Your credit score*

What Is Identity Theft?

Identity theft is a serious crime where someone else uses your personal information (name, social security number, home address, etc.) without your permission to commit fraud or other crimes. The federal government estimates that as many as 9 million American's identities are stolen each year. Identity thieves may use your credit report score and record to rent an apartment, obtain a credit card, open a telephone account, or get approval for a major loan (like a mortgage).

When the identity thief fails to pay for the goods or services he has obtained, default on payments will show up in your credit report. This not only lowers your credit report score, but the creditors will most likely come to you to pay off the debt. People don't usually know this is happening unless they spot an unauthorized charge on a credit card or see unknown credit inquiries and accounts on their credit report.

Some people are able to resolve identity theft problems fairly quickly, but others spend years and thousands of dollars trying to restore their good credit report.

Occurrence and Prevention of Identity Theft

While there are a wide variety of ways thieves get your personal information and steal your identity, here are some of the most common methods:

Identity Theft – Don't Be The Next Victim!

1. Dumpster Diving - *The identity thief goes through your garbage to find bills or other mail with your personal information. One way to prevent this is to shred any paper with your name, address, or any other personal information. Be very careful about what you throw out. Once it's in the garbage, it's an open book.*

2. Skimming - *Some technologically-savvy identify thieves can steal your credit card numbers while they are being processed at the store. This is particularly easy when you make online purchases. While you can't protect yourself from all of these attempts, you can use secure sites when entering credit card or bank information on the internet. Though it's probably not generally approved of, you can easily use false address and telephone numbers to discourage use of your private information. Be sure and check your statements as soon as they come in for unauthorized orders are charges. And if you do much online banking or bill-paying, you can check your accounts regularly online for charges you didn't make. Be careful and cautious in using your IDs and passwords to make purchases or apply for credit on internet sites.*

3. Phishing - *An identity thief may pose as a bank or credit card company and ask you to verify personal information. They may do this through an e-mail that looks as if it has come from a trusted business, through a spammed e-mail asking you to follow an innocent-looking link to their not-so-innocent website, or they may catch you off guard with pop-ups or instant messages requesting personal information. They may even use the telephone to get this information from you. NEVER give your personal information out to anyone you don't know. Before verifying private information with an online service, check to make sure that the company you deal with is really the company that sent the request.*

4. Changing your Address - *Identity thieves have been known to divert mail by submitting a change of address notice with the post office, thereby diverting your personal credit information to them. This is one area where maintaining and* *checking your personal information with companies on the internet may allow you to spot such fraudulent attempts.*

5. Old-fashioned Theft - *Hold on to your wallet, your purse, mail, pre-approved credit offers, checks, or tax information. Once an identity thief has possession of your belongings, they can easily imitate you and abuse your good credit report.*

6. Pretexting - *Another technique that is difficult for you to control is the practices of obtaining your personal information from the companies you deal with. The identity thief may pretend to be conducting research to get information the establishment would not otherwise divulge. Once he has your personal information, he may call your bank, pretending he's lost his checkbook or other important information like your investments. Pretexting is against the law, but you may be the last to know when it's happened.*

The single most important thing you can do to keep your own identity safe is to be aware of all activity on your accounts and to make regular reviews of your credit reports. They will contain the information you need to know if someone else is meddling in your business and using your identity for their benefit. The sooner you know something's going on, the more quickly and

effectively you'll be able to stop it and have your credit reports corrected. Allowing abuse of your credit report to gone on for months or even years can create a serious, costly, and time-consuming

effort to win back your good reputation.

What Should I Look For On My Credit Report For Evidence Of Identity Theft?

Review your credit report carefully as soon as you receive it. Pay close attention to the report of inquiries about your credit. If you have specifically applied for a loan or opened a new account, you should find a credit inquiry from that company.

But additional inquiries may indicate that someone else is making applications using your name and information. If you find such inquiries, immediately contact the inquiring creditor and the credit report agency.

Immediately notify the credit reporting agency if you find errors like a closed account that shows as open or a paid-off balance that appears to be outstanding. You may have to provide documentation to support corrections, and you may have to make the same contact several times to assure the correction is made. But be persistent. Your credit report is a direct reflection of your financial dealings. Creditors and credit report agencies are obligated to report correct information.

Check every credit statement you receive to verify that you know about and approve all charges it contains. Make sure it reflects recent payments, too. Contact the creditor quickly and follow- through to make sure your account information is accurate and up-to-date.

A little common sense and a lot of precaution will help you avoid identity theft and bad credit you didn't earn. Keep up with your accounts. Review credit reports regularly, and be sure to follow- up when they contain errors. You'll find the rewards of your effort in your credit report score!

Protect Your Credit With Identity Theft Shield

Today we live in a world that has become more complicated than it ever was before. Technological innovations allow for us to make business deals in just a short time on the net. However, with this technology comes the risk of cyber-crimes. Identity theft is a common crime today, and it has grown to great proportions mainly due to the digitization age.

The Federal State Commission in the States tells us that there have been over 27 million reports of identity theft since '99, and that in 2003 alone there were 10 million cases. This just tells us that this kind of crime is on the rise.

What next?

Well, you may have had your personal credit card stolen. In a case like this the credit card company or bank can assist you by blocking the card and replacing it with a fresh one. But there is more to identity theft than this simplicity. Have you heard about the identity theft shield?

You can use it when opening a new bank account, applying for a credit card and things like that. It is a kind of insurance against fraud, and we now know we can all be victims of these things.

One may imagine that all you would want, after being a victim of identity theft would be to clear your own name of crimes the thief may have committed under your name. But the legal services departments have worked hard at these issues and things are easier today. For example this company called Kroll has made efforts to assist many companies, to secure people's private data. Such security is required in banks and card companies, since they have a huge database of people's private data. They are the targets of the hackers.

How Identity Shield can help you

Well, you would have quick and fool proof access to your data and your belongings. The shield gives you a credit rating so you can monitor every financial move you make, as well as its affects. It is good for people who use many credit cards to be linked with an identity shield service. It helps them to make regular reports and also give their clients regular updates on their finance, at no additional charge.

The identity shield would warn you if your finances were suddenly in danger, so you do not really have to worry about that.

You would feel free from creditors who would love to make a little more out of you! That is how the shield truly does get its name - it shields you from trouble and disaster.

So if you do feel that your credit record may be in danger, do take the time to have a discussion with a sales rep from an identity theft shield provider. It may just be what saves you from a major hurdle.

Identity Theft Protection And Being Safe Online

If you are a smart consumer, you know that identity theft protection is something you always need to strive for. If you do not do everything that you can to protect yourself from those that are looking to walk away with your identity and more than likely your money, you may be facing years of heart ache and frustration. One of the most common areas that people worry about identity theft in is that of the online world. Each year, thousands of people will face problems with their identity being stolen from the web. To protect yourself, learn what you can do know.

There are several ways in which people can get your information on the web. You may be thinking that you just should not use any of your credit cards online, but this does not have to be the case. You need to use them smartly. Here are some tips to help you to insure that identity theft is not something that happens to you when you are online.

- *Only use your credit card on secure sites. To know if a website is secure, make sure that there is an 's' after the http in the browser box where the website's address is located. A secured site is nearly impossible for someone to steal information from.*

- *Only use your credit card directly from merchants you know. If you want to make a purchase from a merchant that you do not know, you should consider using an e-currency company such as PayPal. This service allows you to hook your credit card or your bank account up to it.*

- *When you want to make a payment online, you can pay with your PayPal account which will then draw the funds from your account. Your account and information does not go to the merchant at all.*

- *Use and run your spyware. In some cases, people may have spyware on their computer. This software gets into your computer through an email download, through a file or program or in several other ways. If the program gets on your computer, it may be able to track and store information about what you are doing (perhaps even your credit card information) on the program and then reports it back without you having any idea. Spyware protection should be on continuously and run at least weekly.*

- *Finally, do not every give out your personal information online, in an email or in a chat room. There is no reason that someone should have your full address, name or credit cards numbers in this means. You need to carefully consider what you are providing so that you do not make the mistake of providing the wrong information to the wrong people.*

Identity theft protection starts in your hands especially online.

How To Prevent Identity Theft When Making Payments Online

When it comes to shopping online, you may think that you should never do it. The fact is, though, that this is the way of the future and you should do it. But, you should be smart about it. This is part of your identity theft protection knowledge. You should always be able to know when it is safe to make a purchase online and when it is not.

- *Always look for the 'S' after the http in the browser window. This S stands for secure. In most cases, this means that others cannot get onto that page to access your information.*

- *Shop from reputable retailers that you know and trust. If you are unsure about one, use an online ecurrency set up instead. For example, use PayPal to make your payments. You can make your payments to them and then use the funds there to pay the company. This keeps your personal information, such as your credit card, safe from those on the web.*

- *Always type in the website address instead of following links that are sent to you. This way, you are sure that you go to the right location instead of going to one that may be a fake set up to look like the original.*

Online identity protection is something that you need to have and do each time that you think about making a purchase on the web.

Protecting Yourself From Identity Theft On The Web

When it comes to making purchases on the web, there are several things that you should know about when it comes to identity theft protection. Several people think that identity theft is something that will happen to them if they make purchases on the web. Yet, what is important to know here is that if you make purchases in the right manner and take care while you are online, you should not have any problems when it comes to doing so. You do not have to feel worried every time you attempt to make a purchase. Just use these tips to help you.

First of all, make sure that the websites that you are visiting allow you to pay for their purchase on a secured webpage. This page should have an address that starts with https. If the s is missing, the site is not secure on the payment page and you should not use it. Secondly, if you an ad comes to you through your email, you should not click on the links in the email to visit the site especially if it is a big, well known company. Instead type it into your browser so that you make sure you are not going to a fake website geared at taking your money.

You should never provide anyone on the web with your personal information either. You can also use a payment service, such as PayPal. This will allow you to make purchases without the worry that more than the purchase price will be applied to your account. This is a great form of protection on the web. Also, make sure that you have an up to date and running spyware program. This will help you to insure that no one is recording your information while you are online and reporting it back.

There are many things that you can do to insure that you are always safe when it comes to making payments and purchase on the web. In fact, you can safeguard your identity in a number of ways here.

Combating Online Identity Theft

How do you like knowing that hackers just sent you a virus? Did you know that there is another way these predators are attacking on the web?

Identity theft is a rapidly growing problem for many people. For several million people, it has already ruined personal transactions.

How can people do this? What are the identity thefts repercussions and what can you do to prevent it?

Identity Theft – Don't Be The Next Victim!

In the United States alone, identity theft is no longer uncommon because several bureaus are taking immediate actions to be rid of this problem. Yet, there is still some difficult in doing so.

Identity theft can happen when a hacker is able to obtain your information via the Internet. Data such as your full name, bank account number(s), and other information that has been posted online. Once they get this information, they are able to use it for many forms of crime. Whether it is to commit fraud or even just to steal your hardworking money.

All you need to do to know you are broke is check your checking account. All your money is gone!

A new way of online identity theft is spoofing. How does spoofing work you ask? Spoofing works by recreating a website with one that has the same name. In other words, that site becomes one the thief takes control of. He is now the head boss and able to control all the finances from the website.

There are three basic parts can let the thief manipulate ID theft. These are: Domain name, actual content and web hosting.

1. Domain Name - These sites can be purchased from numerous online sources for a small price. The name will have dashes, letters and numbers.

2. Actual Content - The second component to start a website. Remember HTML and streaming media. This is the second key module in order to publish a site. The vital factor to deem here is the HTML and the streaming media are needed to distribute online.

3. Web Posting - This is the last step in the hacker's plan to boost his plan off for stealing people's identity. From here, the thief will say that website plus its principals and employees.

With all this, the profits that are supposed to go to the rightful owners will go to the thieves instead. Potential clients and buyers will not even notice the difference.

Individuals and companies do have a way of protecting themselves. Identity thieves can get through many of the blocks that websites put up. Yet, with two different tactics, companies can reduce their chances of being spoofed.

1. It is important to protect yourself so getting an anti-virus program would be the smart thing to do. One major way thieves can get all your information is sending you worms and viruses.

These viruses will compromise your computer and having one of these anti-virus programs to weed them out can help. The more protected you are, the less chance these thieves will get your personal and company information.

2. Secure servers have the ability to transmit data over the website without compromising people's information. Using this can help when people are transmitting credit card information to buy something off your website.

A thing that needs to be looked into before you go with a securing server company, be informed about the business you are going to be paying to secure your information before you give out any online data to them.

Get the things that protect your website for your own sake and the sake of those visiting your site.

Online Identity Theft Protection

As the world becomes more and more dependent on the web, there are increasing amounts of opportunity for identity theft to happen. For those that are using the web to pay for things, this can be one of the most troublesome things. Yet, it is also important to note that online identity theft is about the same risk as it is for those that use a credit card in other venues. The same risk is posed here. Still, knowing how to protect yourself from online identity theft is very important. You should also be teaching your children to do the same thing as it is not always money that these thieves are after.

Basic Information

First and foremost, you should be leery of providing anyone on the web with your personal information. If you are just chatting with someone (even if you think you know them) you should pay special attention to what they are asking you...

For example, you should never provide details about who or where you are. Your address should never be given over the web in an instant message or in a chat room. In fact, probably not in an email either. You should never provide your social security number to anyone either. You should never provide any information about your financial information either. We'll get more into detail about that in just a minute. Make sure that none of this basic information about you is available on profiles either.

Making Payments Online

When it comes to shopping online, you may think that you should never do it. The fact is, though, that this is the way of the future and you should do it. But, you should be smart about it.

This is part of your identity theft protection knowledge. You should always be able to know when it is safe to make a purchase online and when it is not.

- *Always look for the 's' after the http in the browser window. This s stands for secure. In most cases, this means that others cannot get onto that page to access your information.*

- *Shop from reputable retailers that you know and trust. If you are unsure about one, use an online ecurrency set up instead. For example, use PayPal to make your payments. You can make your payments to them and then use the funds there to pay the company. This keeps your personal information, such as your credit card, safe from those on the web.*

- *Always type in the website address instead of following links that are sent to you. This way, you are sure that you go to the right location instead of going to one that may be a fake set up to look like the original.*

Online identity protection is something that you need to have and do each time that you think about making a purchase on the web.

Be Informed and Up-to-Date! Read Articles Concerning

Identity Theft

Online crimes have quickly become common place today. It comes as a nasty surprise to one when you know your password has been hacked into. At times it can cause you monetary loss as well as embarrassment among people, that you have 'sent' emails to.

The internet in itself is a great place to learn more about identity theft. You can find much information on how you can stay protected on the internet, right on the internet!

Stay Informed

Articles that talk about identity theft are probably the best way to get some know-how on this topic. Articles on this subject will inform you as to how exactly a 'thief' can pose as you on the internet to use your identity for their own personal benefit. This is a relatively new form of crime and courts are still deciding on new laws to battle these thieves. You can find a lot of information on existing court cases of identity theft as well.

The different categories

identity theft could be as simple as a friend playing a practical joke, to fool another common friend using your identity - maybe an instant messenger id for example. On the other hand it could be a serious a matter as a complete stranger going to great lengths to find out your ATM pin number, your email passwords, your bank account details, your PayPal id maybe and things like that. When a person cracks one of your passwords, for example your email password, it becomes quite easy for him or her to crack the rest of the information from there. People have lost a lot of money due to such illegal activities, and that is the kind of identity theft you need to protect yourself from.

People who commit such malicious crimes are generally very shrewd minds who get a kick out of it. However when they have access to your personal details, it is only a matter of time before they succumb to using it for their own benefit.

Precaution

Prevention is better than cure, and that is doubly so with the case of online identity theft. You have a fingerprint in the real world, that no one can really fake. On the internet, your passwords are your only fingerprint. Take care of your passwords and never reveal them to any one not even close family.

The most common complaint of identity theft is the misuse of credit cards. When you enter your personal credit card details on a website to genuinely purchase a personal product, you are revealing your personal private details to a third party. It is easy for one of these company employees who are not even a smart mind, to go ahead and use your details to make purchases on your card.

You need articles on the subject to learn more about protecting yourself from identity theft!

Identity Theft Commercials

Many a time people tend to take identity theft commercial very lightly, and at times they find them funny as well. They wouldn't be laughing is such did happen to them, because more often than not, identity theft does involve monetary losses. Then there may be some of these ads that literally scare the living daylights out of you. I believe either of these cases is the undesirable affect. They are supposed to warn you and inform you in an objective manner. Don't take these ads too lightly, neither take them as a fearful idea - but use them to be informed.

The ads that you see on TV are in fact a reflection of what may actually take place around you. It is not a laughing matter at all. In fact many of these ads are effective in warning you of the right way to use your credit card online, and that is the most productive issue about these ads.

Some of the ads are reality oriented, meaning you can see and hear a person who has had a personal experience with identity theft. It is interesting to note that it does happen to the everyday lame Jane, and not just to the big wigs in society. Normally that is enough to make one take notice. When it can happen to the person next to you, it can happen to you as well.

Identity thieves often resort of sneaky means (can there be any other) to get your personal information right from under your nose. They use information like credit card number, social security number and maybe a copy of your birth certificate if they can get their hands on it, to pose as you, online and sometimes in the real world as well.

It is the duty of advertisements on this issue to inform people of some of the strategies made use of by identity thieves to get your personal information. Phishing emails for example are fake emails posing as your bank or other commercial website, asking you for personal information. Once you give it out, if you do, the thief logs in to your bank or website with the details and takes out all your money!

Have you heard about shoulder surfing? Its literally peeping over one's shoulder with a hidden camera, that is. Hidden cameras can record the PIN numbers you enter into an ATM or into your cellular phone. Once the thief can work out the number, guess what happens next! Of late there has been a huge up rise in fraud emails. You get an email stating that you have won a lottery, bagged a great job or something like that. All you need to do is pay the processing fee of a small amount and the rest is all yours. Of course you never hear from them again.

Keep yourself informed about identity theft, by paying due attention to the commercials which have been produced for your benefit.

Identity Theft Videos

Identity theft is rapidly growing to being the worst crime people hear about. It can take place in big cities and little towns.

What is identity theft? It is defined by the as stealing one's identity to use and commit fraud. It is done to rob a person of their money.

To be knowledgeable in what ways a person can steal your identity, how the crime works and how you can prevent it; a video about this crime is your best way to learn about it.

Should you be lucky enough to obtain a copy of the identity theft videotape, share it with friends and family to make them aware of the white collar crime. It is important that everyone knows about this crime because the hassle that goes along with it is something no one should have to go through.

The video will demonstrate six steps that thieves use to steal your data and your identity. This video should be a top priority for those wanting to know more about identity thieves.

- Dumpster Diving

By rummaging through your garbage, thieves can often times obtain your information. It is important for you to be rid of those documents that contain both personal and financial data carefully. If you do not have a shredder machine, burning the document as well as shredding it by hand can help curb this type of thieving.

- Stealing your wallet or purse

This is the most common way a person can steal one's identity. What you may think as a common theft could turn quickly into identity theft. To avoid being a victim in two ways, keep your belongings close to you in public.

Should you become a victim, remember that all your bank information is in your possession, contact your credit card carrier as well as your bank to inform them of the loss.

- Online scams

Thieves will try and compromise your data by sending you emails that offer prizes or other neat offers. They will ask you information like your full name, address, credit card number and other personal information for you to obtain what they have for you. Do not give them this information. The majority of these emails are scams.

- Snail Mail

Thieves do not mind going through your mail after the mailman or mailwoman delivers it. They don't mind getting your information this way. If possible, try to get the mail shortly after it has been delivered.

- Your Home

If a thief wants to break into your home to steal much needed documents for identity theft, there really isn't anything stopping them. This includes you being in your home. However, getting a secure lock as well as getting your neighbors to look after it can help if you and your family are gone.

- Filling Out Documents

A thief will take pride in looking over your shoulder as you fill out documents for just about anything including credit or other things. Fill out the information in a more secluded place.

Once the thieves have your data, they can use it in five different ways. The video will explain how.

- Open a new credit card account in your name

- Purchase a new vehicle in your name with an auto loan

- Should they be arrested, they will give the police your name instead of their own. Should they be released and not show up, a warrant will be issued in your name.

- They can open up new bank accounts in your name and write bad checks.

- They can call your credit card company pretending to be you and change the address on your file.

What To Do When Id Theft Occurs

All right, so it happened. Even with all of the precautions and care you've taken to protect yourself from those spineless and despicable thieves, somehow and someway they found a way to the inside...to the inside your personal and financial life that i.

Now don't be too hard on yourself.

I know that you're saying to yourself right now, "I did everything I could possibly do. I took the time to make myself aware and educate myself on the facts and this still happened...why?"

Well, unfortunately sometimes there is no real answer to the question why, it just is what it is. You have to keep in mind that these perpetrators are professionals and they will stop at nothing to achieve their goal.

Just like you go to work every day and perform your job with the proficiency and skills that you have acquired, so do they. Their job every day is to rip off honest, hardworking and innocent people such as you and I. It's not fair and it never will be. They have made a huge mess of your life and you are the one who is stuck with the task of picking up the pieces and turning things right again. Sometimes you can build that fence higher, make the bridge more difficult to cross and even fill the moat with alligators, but inevitably there will always remain a weak and penetrable spot. Identity thieves are adept at looking for and seeking out those particular spots. The most important thing for you to keep in mind right now is that regardless of how much damage was done and how bad the situation looks at present, it could always be worse. Think about what would have happened had you not already been so familiar with how identity theft works. You may not have been able to prevent it but you certainly knew how to recognize the fact that it was happening to you.

The signs were there and you didn't just dismiss them, as many others would have this early in the process.

Maybe you noticed that your credit card statements had not arrived at the time of month that they generally should have. Perhaps during regular review of your bank statements you noticed some unusual transactions that you had not made.

Your Liability As A Victim Of Identity Theft

The question you have probably been asking yourself throughout this entire book is…"What is my liability in this situation"?

Identity Theft – Don't Be The Next Victim!

Well unfortunately that answer is fairly complex and is dependent on the type of identity theft that has occurred, as well as the timeliness in which you have responded and taken action to correct the problem. In some cases, victims are able to identify and act on the problem quickly resulting in very minimal financial loss. Other particular situations have not worked out quite so well and have resulted in substantial financial debt and a very poor credit rating, which can take years and years to repair.

Let me tell you about a few specific cases of identity theft in where the victim truly ended up as the injured party in more ways than one.
Actual Identity Theft Victim Cases

A gentleman in San Diego, California (we'll call him John Jones), encountered an identity thief who opened a PayPal account under John's name and filtered $7,600 from John's Bank of America account into the forged PayPal account. The incident occurred during July and August of 2002 but because John had been traveling he did not notice the money was actually missing until January of 2003.

He contacted his bank and was informed that because he had failed to notify the bank within 60 days of the occurrence there was nothing they could do for him. By that time all of the money, with the exception of $2,100 still remaining in the PayPal account had been spent. PayPal returned the remaining sum to John but he was still out $5,000. John sued both PayPal and Bank of America in small claims court, pleading that PayPal should have notified him immediately upon discovering the fraud. Bank of America counter argued that it is the customer's responsibility to regularly check bank statements and ensure their accuracy. In the end John walked away with a settlement from each of the firms, however was still out approximately $500 as a result. His yearlong battle to turn things right was extensive, time consuming and frustrating.

Identity Theft Protection: How To Get Help

If you feel that you may be a victim of identity theft, then you may be facing a situation that you just do not know what to do in. The fact is, though, that this type of threat can happen to anyone at virtually anytime. You do not need to do anything wrong, per se, to have something go wrong for you. When you think that someone has violated your personal information, you should take action immediately to begin fixing the damage that they may have caused you.

Where To Start

First, determine what has been violated. If you are missing your credit card, driver's license or any other type of financial or identification item, you should call and have them canceled right away. This way, they are locked out the system and cannot be used. You should also talk to your credit card lender to find out if anyone has put any charges on your credit card that may not have been yours. You should work with them to find out how you need to go about getting your identity theft protection on your credit cards into gear so that you are not responsible for those charges any longer.

Next, check your credit report. Your credit report is a very important piece of paper (actually most will get theirs on the web these days.) In any case, you need to insure that the information that is being reported there about you is actually accurate. This way, you will know that the identity is still safe and has not been stolen. If you find errors on your credit report, especially those that have to do with an account that you possibly did not open. If you find these things listed on your credit report, you may be a victim of identity theft. Also, make sure to look that there are no wrong addresses listed for you either. You should insure this because others at that address may be using your information to secure their own lines of credit.

If you find errors on your credit report, there are several things that you need to do. First, you need to call the lenders that are listed (the credit agency will provide you with their numbers) and find out what the account in question is and inform them that you did not open it. Then, you will need to work with them to determine what the right information is. From here, you will need to talk to your credit agencies and have them clear up any discrepancies that are listed there. You may need to work with an attorney to help you to get through all of the paperwork.

Always take care when it comes to your identity theft protection so that you know that the best opportunities are available to you.

Being An Identity Theft Victim Is Not Easy

In a 2004 study, the Ways and Means Committee of the U.S. House of Representatives reported that, in 2003 alone, almost 10 million Americans had become victims of identity theft. The crime cost consumers about $5 billion out-of-pocket and costs American business around $50 billion. As increasing news reports indicate, identity theft is the crime of the era. It's increasing rapidly. Unfortunately, it's also a difficult crime to catch and prosecute.

In 2003, victims of identity theft spent anywhere from $500 to $1200 and from 30 to 60 hours of their personal time trying to resolve the financial problems created by identity theft. Further, the crime itself occurred over a three- to six-month period in each known case.

We all hope we never become victims of identity theft.

For one thing, you usually don't learn you're a victim until some debt collector calls you about a bill or a loan application is denied because of your poor credit history or low credit score.

This news comes as a shocking surprise to most victims of identity theft, and the personal agony of financial loss and effort needed to resolve the problem take a huge toll. Identity theft victims often report they feel as violated as they would if they had been mugged or their house had been burglarized.

Today, prevention and early detection are best solutions to the identity theft problem. These criminals have a variety of ways to get your personal financial information. They may steal it from your garbage in the form of old bills or pre-approved credit offers. They may trick you on the phone or by e-mail into giving out your personal information. Someone you know and trust may have access to your personal information. Or perhaps someone with good eyesight is standing behind you, watching you enter your PIN at the ATM machine or grocery counter. These things are within your control, but there are other tactics outside your control. Identity thieves also trick the information out of banks and businesses, claiming they are research for a non-existent company or using false identities to secure the information. Hackers may sneak into the databases of large companies and download the information they keep for their clientele.

Once they have your personal information, they can submit false address change reports to your bank or creditors. They can apply for mortgages or loans or make purchases against your credit cards. You won't know about it until the *#(& hits the fan, and your credit history is ruined.

How Can I Tell If Someone Is Using My Personal Financial Information Illegally?

So how do you know that an identity thief may be targeting your personal information? What
are the signs to look for? And what do you do if you think you are a victim of identity theft? Here are a few of the things you can watch for to protect your personal financial information and your identity:

1. *Order a credit report, at the very least, once a year. If a close review of your credit report reveals accounts you've never heard of or loans you did not make, you may be a victim. The report could also contain inquiries about your credit from merchants and vendors you didn't apply to. These are all important red flags, and you should follow-up on the information immediately.*

2. *You receive a bill or statement from a company you didn't open an account with.*

3. *You notice unauthorized or incorrect changes on your credit card or bank statement.*

4. *You get calls from business owners or debt collectors who claim you have a bill that is overdue for a product or service you never ordered or received.*

5. *You are denied approval of a loan or credit card application, even when you know your credit is good.*
If you've noticed any of these warning signs, follow up immediately by contacting the credit card company, bank, or credit report agency with questions. Don't accept inadequate answers to your questions. And continue to follow-up until all your questions have been answered and your credit account or report is accurate and up-to-date.

If you find you can't resolve issues easily, you may be an identity theft victim already. Report this problem to law enforcement authorities immediately. Contact your bank, your creditors, and the credit report agencies to let them know the problem is occurring and ask them to freeze your accounts. Add special passwords that anyone inquiring about our using your accounts must know to get a transaction approved. Do what you can to find out what the identity thief has done.

For example, where have they opened accounts or where have the applied for loans. Can you find another address associated with your name that is not familiar to you? If you identify the identity thief, do not contact them directly. Rather provide that information to law enforcement.

Identity Theft Reporting

7 Reasons Why You Should Use This

Identity theft as we know is on the rise. It is through measures like reporting it that we can battle this growing menace here's how you can help. It has prevailed (id theft) through efforts by governments and individuals alike. The internet has only made it easier for the hackers to get access to all your personal information under one roof - your email id.

The government of United States has called for seven preventive methods to curb this growing menace. If not prevent it altogether, it will at least prevent further misuse of your identity, if you follow these seven steps.

1. Get in touch with the department of fraud in the government, when you have a fraud alert. The fraud alert is of course a personalized data that you use when you work with an office that deals with it. If and when the department comes across a double identity - it reports you of it immediately. This is a great way to curb the menace of identity theft, and if you are lucky you may even nab the culprit.

2. if you have reason to believe that your identity has been stolen, get into immediate contact with the nearest police station or sheriff's office. If you wait too long to do this you are ruining chances of catching the culprit and it could lead to further loss if it involves something like your credit card.

3. When you are talking to the police personnel, or narrating the incident for reasons of their report making, be as objective as possible. Do not leave out any

details but do not go off the track as well. This will be the report that the office will use to begin an investigation, so it better be good!

4. Get in touch with your bank to cancel all credit cards and to issue new ones, and they may need the police report for this. So make sure you carry a copy of the report when you meet with the bank officials. The bank will decide on what measures need to be taken to provide you with future service. In most cases they will immediately suspend the account. Following this, they may issue you a whole new account number and new cards as well. You will probably be charged a fee for this, but that is the least of your problems!

5. If money has been withdrawn from your account before you realized there was a theft, let your bank know about it immediately. This information could give them the chance to trace the location where it was withdrawn, and take everyone closer to getting the bad guy.

6. Let the check verification agency know about this theft. They could stop payments on checks.

7. In any case, it is better to notify the social security office and get a whole new security number.

Following these seven steps will get you out of the mess.

Fraud Alert - Take the Power out of Identity Thieves' hands

The one thing a person can't take from you is your self-respect and the one thing that you are proud of is your self-identity. Your self-identity is your individual difference from everyone else. Your person reflects the being you are and who you will be as well as your personality. Your uniqueness from all others. All this... this cannot be taken from you.

In saying this... people can steal your identity nowadays. They can't take your personality but they can try and be you.

Should you be alarm? You better believe it! The American dream is one everyone wants to touch and have. Yet, some people do not want to work for it. They want it at someone else's expense. They will get that American dream they want so badly even at your price.

The kicker of this problem is when someone's identity is taken and used for criminal acts. Imagine you are driving in your road and you get pulled over... maybe for speeding, maybe the cop ran your tag but you get pulled over. Your name is mixed up with someone who didn't show up for court on a weapons charge or burglary charge. Do you think it will be easy to prove that you are not the person they think you are? It may be your name but it isn't you. This is a violation of your person.

How did these people do this to you? Somehow they were able to retrieve your social security number, address, name, date of birth and bank account data.

Are these thieves getting joy and benefit from taking things from you? You can bet they are. People who steal others identities are making a huge profit off of your good name.

Another example: a person has just obtained information about your banking institute including your account number and even your routing number.
He or she can then take all that money and transfer the funds to another bank or begin purchasing items. All without having to worry about walking into the bank. That is scary, huh?

Get a Fraud Alert Placed On Your Credit Report

So how do you protect your good name, credit and finances? One way to protect it is to get a fraud alert placed on your credit report. This is a way to get the credit bureaus aware of any possible issues. Fraud alerts can stop thieves from getting credit. Should someone try, the credit bureau will call you right away about it.

If for some reason, you cannot be reached, the credit will not be issued in your name and this warns the credit companies trying to obtain it that you have not authorized any type of transaction to go on.

How to Set Up a Fraud Alert

Believe it or not, this is one of the easiest things to get to protect your credit. Just work together with the credit bureau fraud alert department to get it all set up. Get your file top flagged and by recording your voice in the response system, it will be a way to identify if you made the attempt to get credit.

Should you wish to remove the alert at any given time... you can do so by writing the credit bureaus and informing them.
Know this that some creditors will not authorize credit if a fraud alert was placed even with good intentions.

Fraud alerts are one of your best weapons against identity theft and thieves but take other precautions like protecting your social security number for one.

How To Report Identity Theft

Identity theft. What is this that everyone once said was a victimless crime? It is the act of stealing a person's identity including their name, address, phone number, credit cards and even their mother's maiden name.

There is no particular one person that cannot be a victim of identity theft. Everyone meets the requirements. College students, children and even businesses can all be a victim of fraud. Once you have been victimized, there are things you need to do for proper interventions.

You should know who stole your personal information from the computer and opened new accounts without your permission. The sooner this is done, the better to avoid any other repercussions.

Established in 2005, an identity theft law was changed to stipulate that anyone can get their credit report once a year free of charge. Whenever a person is denied credit, they have up to 60 days to get a credit report.

This can help them determine why they were denied. It is usually here that people often find out they have been a victim of fraud.

With a monthly review possible, it is more probable that someone will catch unauthorized charges and credit on their report. With early intervention, it is possible to get your credit protected with fraud alerts placed on all three of your reports. All creditors will need to contact you before any credit is issued in your name. There are also smaller services that offer to monitor your credit report for a small monthly fee.

What do you do if your identity has already been stolen? The first thing to do is report it to your local police department although you'll be jumping through hoops and cutting through the red tape to even get a statement taken. This leaves many people will a bad taste in their mouth and a discontent feeling. Secondly, get a fraud alert placed on your file especially if you haven't done so yet.

Police have not caught up to technological times when it comes to identity theft. They have no active role and cannot give proper advice in what to do. There is so much paperwork that will need to be completed. It will be these that you will send to companies and agencies responsible for giving out the credit in the first place.

So if the police are no good in helping and there isn't much you can do beforehand, then what can you do and where can you go to report the crime? Not only that but do you know who stole your identity... do you have that kind of information to fill out the forms? If so, where would you send those kind of forms?

You will have to go through lots of red tape just to clear your name. It's a mess that you did not create but have to contend with. It can cause many headaches.

While there are many numbers on the federal and state agencies level, it is important to get into contact with them. Depending on the jurisdiction and the type of crime committed, the Federal Trade Commission or the FTC can help in cases such as these.

It will not happen overnight but you can clear your credit and good name. As soon as you know it happened, you need to start contacting people and businesses. Credit bureaus, agencies, companies and investigators will help to weed out the errors on your report.

For your information: Keep all relevant information and files of the situation in a safe folder. Make sure you write down times you have talked with people.

Actual Identity Theft Victim Cases

A gentleman in San Diego, California (we'll call him John Jones), encountered an identity thief who opened a PayPal account under John's name and filtered $7,600 from John's Bank of America account into the forged PayPal account. The incident occurred during July and August of 2002 but because John had been traveling he did not notice the money was actually missing until January of 2003. He contacted his bank and was informed that because he had failed to notify the bank within 60 days of the occurrence there was nothing they could do for him. By that time all of the money, with the exception of $2,100 still remaining in the PayPal account had been spent. PayPal returned the remaining sum to John but he was still out $5,000. John sued both PayPal and Bank of America in small claims court, pleading that PayPal should have notified him immediately upon discovering the fraud. Bank of America counter argued that it is the customer's responsibility to regularly check bank statements and ensure their accuracy. In the end John walked away with a settlement from each of the firms, however was still out approximately $500 as a result. His yearlong battle to turn things right was extensive, time consuming and frustrating.

An elderly woman in Seattle, Washington (we'll call her Jane Doe), was the victim of a telemarketing scam in December of last year. Jane provided her checking account information to the caller and later found that her account had been cleaned of $800, leaving her overdrawn by $300. When her December Social Security check was deposited the Bank of America withdrew $300 of it to cover the overdraft.

Jane was left with barely enough money for food and rent and was forced to "skip" Christmas that year. By February the Bank of America had returned some of the money to her and was continuing to work with her to repair the situation.

The Moral Behind Every Identity Theft Stories

It is shocking to hear so many horror stories being told from the victims of identity theft. Should things continue the way they are, you can be sure to see and hear more terrifying crimes of people being victimized.

Recent studies show that seven million people plus have fallen victim to the crime. This is just in the United States. If you were to enter this data enter a computer and have it compute it, this is 19,000 cases a day.

With these numbers, it should be assumed that identity theft is given real attention but it isn't. Yet, it should always be given serious attention and have more focused poured to it. With technology advancing further, more stories of identity theft are not likely to end anytime soon.

The paragraphs above were just summaries but if you compare them to the actual life stories of victims, these may seem insignificant. For those who have suffered the crime can develop a trauma that is not easy to get past. Then hearing more about the stories behind this crime is a bit different than if someone you know or yourself can relate to what has happened.

Despite any prevention measures a person takes, there is no way to stop from becoming a victim to identity theft. Yet, there are measures that can stop the crime from getting worse. It really just takes keep a constant eye on your credit report. Common sense and your instincts will help tell you if something is going off kilter.

When you take these issues into consideration, it does make it much harder for ID thieves to get past the barriers you put into place. You won't be a victim should you take necessary precautions against those who are now dealing with the ID theft after effects.

Remember this phrase: Thieves do not want to work hard to get information. They do not like to work hard at all. If a person makes it hard for them to get credit or information, then it makes it harder for them to make you a victim and move on to another person who may have more relaxed protection.

Example: In the Case of Phishing

This type of criminal contact is done by simply receiving an e-mail that resembles a message that would come from your bank saying your online account was being compromised and confirmation of details need to be sent. There would be a link that is included in the e-mail for convenience. Yet, this link would send you to a fraudulent website. This is called phishing.

No sooner than you click the link, the identity thieves will get a recording of your ID and password. Once that have it, they can access your account and clear it out in just a space of five minutes. You are now not only broke but have been a victim of identity theft.

Making sense out of a confusing situation

Remember that your banks already have this information...all your personal data is saved. If they didn't have it, how could they process your account? They won't be asking for it.

The thing to do is delete the message and do not even put a second thought on it. Should it be legitimate, your bank will try to contact you another way.

Yet, should you have second thoughts, go ahead and delete the message but contact your banking institute. Ask them if they did in fact send the e-mail and why.

Moral of the story... use your instincts before clicking on any link regarding personal information.

What Identity Theft Resource Centers Can Teach You

The crime of identity theft gets increasing attention. In 2005, ABC News conducted a poll that indicated consumer concerns about identity theft had risen sharply. They reported that, in 1998, fewer than 40% of U.S. adults were concerned about identity theft. By 2005, over 70% of all adults were worried that their personal information could be stolen through the internet. In 2006, over 90% of all New York voters were concerned about identity theft.

The news media, which is one of the most effective ways to learn about identity theft, is doing their job - at least as far as publicizing the degree of concern about identity theft. They have also been a good source of information about how individual consumers can prevent theft of their own personal and financial information.

In an era when electronic communications and the internet are making personal information easier to store and transmit, we are likely to continue to see increases in the number of crimes committed against unsuspecting consumers and wary businesses. The frequency of news stories reporting a companies' failure to protect their customers' information makes it clear that consumers and businesses alike are vulnerable to theft of personal information.

Identity Theft – Don't Be The Next Victim!

Today's businesses that maintain databases of customers, their purchases, and their payments must be increasingly vigilant to protect that information from improper sharing and use. Although all big business is vulnerable, the most threatened sectors today are banking and lending institutions, real estate companies, facility management companies, and related fields. E- security becomes a bigger part of their operating costs every year, and the need for such security is supporting the growth of a new employment sector in the U.S. and abroad.

Responding as quickly as they can, both federal and state governments have passed or are working on updating laws that protect personal financial information and impose harsher penalties for the crime of identity theft. However, it is difficult to detect identity theft crimes while they are underway, and it is even more difficult to identify and catch the criminals responsible. A few identity thieves are even using their false documentation to conduct other crimes and escape prosecution.

New and different measures can be seen in the way credit and other financial transactions are done. One new protection is the "security freeze" that allows people to thwart access to their credit report without specific permissions. Consumers must request the freeze from each of the three major credit reporting services. Companies are allows to charge a fee of $10 for this service, but senior citizens older than 64 years and persons who are victims of identity theft are exempt from this charge.

Computer and internet security continues to be a major issue for businesses, especially when they want to attract customers. Advertising increasingly describes tough security measures and assures personal privacy in an attempt to address public concerns about identity theft. Programmers and software developers are working hard in a number of areas to create hack- proof solutions to the problem of identity theft.

For small companies and individuals, the use of removable storage devices like CDs and external hard drives are a practical security solution. But for large companies with thousands to millions of accounts, sophisticate large-scale solutions like firewalls, fingerprinting, and random PIN generators maybe more cost effective. Computer encryption, though a mystery to many of us, is relied on more and more by business to protect sensitive data and personal information.

In today's news-rich environment, it should be clear that the crime of identity theft is still on the rise. Certainly, more people are aware of and concerned about it than ever before. And so far, law enforcement has not been able to catch up with technology. Identity thieves are ahead of
the curve today. But this could change rapidly with the development of new automated solutions and enhanced security practices.

Very recently, FOX News reported that peer-to-peer network file sharing is critical internet security vulnerability, despite the rising popularity of these networks. According to the FOX News article, Mary Engle of the Federal Trade Commission said, "The danger here is clear, as it is commonly acknowledged that criminals now troll file sharing networks for the sole purpose of finding sensitive data that can be used to commit identity theft." But fortunately, Ms. Engle reported, a new security software called Identity Finder helps users find personal financial information within files, e-mails, and web browsers and then enables individuals to delete or protect the data using encryption.

To learn more about identity theft and how to prevent it, visit the Identity Theft Assistance Center (ITAC) on the internet at www.identitytheftassistance.org/. ITAC is a non-profit group of financial service companies dedicated to help identity theft victims by reducing delays and frustration associated with restoring their personal financial integrity and identity. ITAC offers service for victims without charge, helping them inspect their credit reports for signs of identity theft and alerting consumers and businesses to possible fraudulent actions.

In addition, ITAC is sharing this information with state and federal law enforcement in an attempt to help catch and prosecute the responsible criminals.

Identity Theft And Assumption Deterrence Act: Basic Provisions You Need To Know

Did you know that somebody by the name of Terry Rogan was arrested five times for robbery and murder, and that he was in fact an innocent man? The story begins when a convict called Mc Kandes escapes from prison. He already has a copy of Terry's birth certificate. Using this, he creates a fresh bank account, and gets a new drivers' license as well. McKandes is now officially Tery Rogan! He commits robbery and even murder. He does this under the name of Terry, who is duly arrested time and again for crimes he didn't commit. Luckily the fingerprints couldn't match the crime scenes, and Terry was left unaffected, at least not majorly. Terry faced these problems for over three years, until the police finally worked out what was going on.

It can clearly be seen by this example that identity theft is nothing very new, as is often believed. There is a lot that can be accomplished by the copy of your birth certificate in the wrong hands, and that is exactly what did happen to Terry Rogan. This is a crime which can happen against any innocent individual and the sneakiness of the whole thing is what is most scary to people.

You are a sitting duck and attracting such thieves if you have a personal web page that displays all of your information on the net, such as birth date, anniversary dates, and email id - all under one roof!

The Theft and Assumption Deterrence Act

Thanks to the rising alarming numbers of cases of identity theft, the US government passed this law that was signed and acknowledged by the then president Bill Clinton (1998).

This act makes it a federal offence to knowingly pass off as someone else, using any of the means possible including a fake drivers' license, a fake email id or a stolen credit card pin for that matter. Before the act was in place, federal laws only defined the creation of the deceptive act. With this act, we define the real theft in detail.

The age of information was in need of such a law to protect people from online crimes. Courts can today proceed with online identity theft much quicker, thanks to this act. Apart from defining the sentence terms for various degrees of identity theft, the act also speaks of aid to the victims of such a crime. It is true that the inclusion of such an act does not directly prevent the theft of identity over the internet. But it is true that the presence of this act leads to faster court proceedings and accurate and quick sentences. The court cases that had piled up during the nineties, concerning identity theft were sorted out thanks to this law. This serves as a great example to deter thieves from using this route. It is no longer something you can get away with and leave people wondering what went wrong.

The Benefits Of Identity Theft Insurance

In today's world, identity theft is among the fastest growing types of crime in the UK and America. In fact statistics tell us that it happens once every three minutes in the United States! In the United Kingdom about a hundred thousand cases are reported every year. Most people are not too concerned about this whole business - until it happens to them!

What does it mean?
When an imposter deliberately uses your personal details for his or her own benefit, we call this a theft of identity.

It may be something like your social security number, your credit card pin, your bank account number, your birth certificate or even your mother's name! If a person uses your personal details, he takes on your identity.

For example if he uses your social security number to identify himself on the internet, any crime he commits on the internet will be traced back to you and not to the thief. There have been cases in the States where people have been wrongly arrested for the crime someone else committed simply because the guilty was using an innocent man's drivers' license.

Identity theft has not been commonly used for the purpose of terrorism, but it could be. Any crime that a person commits when under your identity is inevitably traced back to you. It could soon become the way of espionage and terrorism.

Once the theft does occur, even if the person who used your identity is caught, you will spend many unhappy and irritating moments trying to convince people 'it wasn't you who did it'.
What you can do about it

Well, prevention surely is better than cure, where identity theft is concerned. Insurance policies against this are probably the best route to take. After all, this IS theft we are talking about. When you can insure your car and your belongings against theft, why not your identity? Of course insurance cannot prevent the theft, but it sure can help you back on your feet if and when the need arises.

When looking to take an identity theft policy, follow the five golden rules:

1. Know exactly what the policy states, word for word and the fine print as well.

2. Make inquiries about deductibles

3. *Keep in mind that this insurance usually does not cover direct losses to finances. Speak to your agent about this, and if he speaks against this statement, he is probably just out to sell you a policy by saying anything he pleases to!*

4. *Do check out all limits of the policy - check if the policy covers salary loss due to identity theft*
- this is the most important to you.

5. *Verify if the legal fee is included in the policy or will you have to shell out towards investigations to the identity theft.*

Federal Law On Identity Theft

Did you know that more people are affected by identity theft than most other crimes put together? How aware of identity theft are you? Did you know this crime is done maliciously?

In the United States alone, this is the fastest growing crime. In 2002, the Federal Trade Commission or simply put the FTC reported 43 percent of the fraud complaints they received where for identity theft. With the 2003 report, the incidents reached close to 10 million.

For every five families, there is always one who will fall prey to these thieves. It is hard not to be a victim even when every precaution in the book has been taken. Even though it seems you have safe guarded your data, the thieves always manage to stay a step ahead.

Understand that everything you do leaves a trail. Whether you use your pin number, write a check, sign up for a credit card or even order something online, thieves, if they want, will get your information.

No matter how hard you try, there lurks the possibility that existing information can still find their way to the identity thieves. Be aware of this fact and cautious with whom you give your vital data out to. Knowing this tactic, can put you above those who just give out their information.

It has been estimated that people spend approximately $500 and more than 30 hours to resolve. Some cases begin from a credit getting
stolen to a person's identity being completely "kidnapped". These crimes are hard to prevent. Because of this, identity theft is hard to correct.

Identity theft is considered a white collar crime. It is because the thieves get in touch with the person directly to steal the information by deception and lies. They will also try and get any money from them that they can.

This crime does not need face to face contact for the thief to steal your identity or your cash. The ID theft is not committed just for the sake of having it but rather using it for other criminal means including to commit fraud.

Until 1998, the federal law had not caught up with this type of crime. In fact, it wasn't until that year, that cases of a bigger magnitude started to show up. It was then that people began to see they needed a heavier sentence imposed on those who committed the fraud in the first place.

Thanks to these numerous cases, the laws were changed so some of these could be used as prosecuting the thieves. Some were changed or enhanced to repair their credit reports or recoup their losses and reputations.

The primary identity theft statute is 18 U.S.C. § 1028(a) (7) enacted on October 30, 1998. This became part of the Identity Theft and Assumption Deterrence Act (or rather the Identity Thief Act.) This act showed support to gain understanding about identity theft and increase the offense of the ID theft acts. Before only 18 U.S.C. § 1028 addressed the fraud creation such as documentation or other personal data.

Identity Theft Act also added §1028(a) (7). which made it a crime to commit fraud with the stolen data. It basically states that any unlawful use without authority is a crime.

The act made is possible for a review and amendment in the Sentencing Guidelines and any penalties that would be imposed for such crime under section 1028.

The federal government established (18 U.S.C. § 1028(a) (7)) to punish identity thieves. This law was designed to help victims get help in prosecuting thieves.

Identity Theft Laws And The People

Have you ever felt pity for those who have suffered from the effects of identity theft? Should you be in their same situation suffering from identity theft, your life may be like theirs and you would understand and feel pity. It is this reason here that laws were passed to detour this continuous threat of security to everyone in the country including business and individuals.

Consumers' awareness to this threat has finally peaked within the last five to ten years.
Largely due to the media attention it has gotten, people are more aware of when they give out their personal data and especially when it is given out without their consent, such is the case on the Internet.

Identity Theft – Don't Be The Next Victim!

With the widespread attention and public outcry, federal and state legislation have been brought up regarding Identity theft issues.

ID Theft and Assumption Law

On the federal level, the Identity Theft and Assumption Deterrence Act (18 USC 1028) was passed in 1998. When the law passed, it made any type of identity theft a felony. The law states that if a person knowingly uses the identification of another person with the sole purpose to commit some type of unlawful crime under both the state and federal laws.

Those who, in turn, violated this law, were put under close supervision by several federal agencies including:

- U.S. Secret Service
- the Social Security Administration
- the Federal Bureau of Investigations (FBI)
- the U.S Postal Service

Criminals were then prosecuted by:

- the U.S. Department of Justice.

The law does allow for victims to be reimbursed. This reimbursement was established within the
Federal Trade Commission as an identity theft clearinghouse.

Following on the federal law's heels, 40 states have criminalized identity theft, most of them being a felony.

Senate Bill 2328 called the Identity Theft Prevention Act of 2000 signed by Sen. Feinstein, Keel and Grassley. They wanted more attention to direct on prevention matters before theft occurs. They wanted also to find out where the prevention should be taken and where the preventions should belong.

President George W. Bush signed the Identity Theft Penalty Enhancement Act or ITPEA as an addition to many of these laws.

What are the provisions of this identity theft law?

When a theft is found to have occurred, it is made a felony with a mandatory two-year sentence in prison. Should any of the theft be related to terrorist activity, there will be an additional five years tacked on.

It also orders the U.S. Sentencing Commission to strengthen its penalties should the theft be found in the role regarding employment.

Many people are happy that identity theft is now being prosecuted but still say the credit bureaus and the industry itself has to make necessary changes before all is said and done.
Laws were also needing to address the frustration that victims felt and a way to for them to let others know they have criminal record that is not theirs.

Some bills that were passed include a provision, which made it possible for people to get contents regarding their own information that has been put together by information broker, employment background checks and an individual reference service.

For those who had criminal records that are not of their own doing, there must be a way for those people to clear it up an expedited process. These would involve the law enforcement where the arrest was first made and the court issues the warrant. Currently, there is no such remedy for
victims of identity theft with criminal records.

On Identity Theft Court Cases: Become More Aware Of Identity Theft

Not that long ago, people didn't worry much when they lost a credit card or threw away a bill. They knew they could contact their creditors and straighten it out pretty quickly. But today, you may be a victim of identity theft and not even know it. This malicious crime is also hard to prosecute because it's difficult to identify and track down the perpetrator.

In 2004, the U.S. House of Representatives Ways and Means Committee issued a report with some surprising statistics about identity theft. They estimated that about 27 million Americans were victims of identity theft from 1999-2004. Half of them didn't know how the thief had gotten their personal information, although a quarter of them knew that the identity theft resulted from a lost or stolen credit card, checkbook, social security number, or personal mail. A few of the victims even reported that the identity thief had used their personal information to carry out a crime under a false identity.

In 2003, the Federal Trade Commission said that reports of identity theft were up 33% from the year before, that they were aware of over 200,000 cases of identity theft in 2003. States with the most reported cases of identity theft were Arizona, Nevada, California, Texas, and Florida. And for almost three quarters of the fraud cases reported, the use of victims' personal information was used for credit card, phone or utility, or bank fraud.
They also found that, on average, the misuse of victims' personal information lasted from three to six months and resulted in a total loss of about $5 billion to victims, plus over 300 million hours of personal time resolving the problems once discovered.

The 2003 FTC Survey reported over $50 billion in losses to business as a result of identity theft. They also reported that, in that year, each victim spent from

$500 to $1200 and from 30 to 60 personal hours to have their credit problems resolved. Unfortunately, there is little hope that this trend will decrease in the near future. Identity theft seems to be getting easier, not harder, and the criminals are learning how to hide their crimes from victims longer and to hide their person from law enforcement altogether.

Unfortunately, there is no single database in the U.S. covering identity theft cases, and the Committee suspects that the number of crimes are vastly underreported. Classifying these crimes as identity theft varies from state to state and from police department to police department. The 2003 study revealed that 60% of victims of identity theft had not reported the crime to their police department! Only one in five had even reported the problem to their credit bureau.

Identity theft crimes are investigated at the federal level by federal agencies like the Secret Service and the FBI. The Department of Justice usually prosecutes the cases through a local U.S. Attorneys' office. In 2000, U.S. Attorneys reported that they had filed over 2000 cases of identity theft across the country (compare this to the 9 million victims per year). That year, the Secret Service made over 3000 arrests, and average actual loses to victims in cases that were closed equaled over $46,000 each. The FBI reported 1425 convictions for identity theft, over a thousand of those for bank fraud. The Postal Inspection Service made a little over 1700 arrests in 2000.

Even the IRS reported actual and suspected cases of identity theft in questionable tax returns in 2000, estimating that they had received around 150 thousand fraudulent returns and fraudulent claims for more than $750 million in refunds. Today, the federal government recognizes that identity theft is the fastest-growing financial crime in America.

One reason for the apparently low proportion of prosecutions and convictions for identity theft has been the government's inability to define the specific crimes. In

Identity Theft – Don't Be The Next Victim!

1998, Congress passed the first law addressing identity theft, the Identity Theft and Assumption Deterrence Act, making identity theft a named federal crime and making it a little easier to prosecute. The Act made the Federal Trade Commission responsible for receipt of complaints and public education about identity theft.

The Identity Theft Penalty Enhancement Act of 2004 established penalties for aggravated identity theft, including those instances where identity theft was used to commit more serious crimes. The Fair and Accurate Credit Transactions Act of 2003 amended the Fair Credit Reporting Act to address identity theft and related consumer issues, making it possible for victims to work with creditors and credit bureaus to remove negative information due to identity theft in their credit report. The Internet False Identification Act of 2000 amended the older False Identification Crime Control Act of 1982 to encompass computer-aided false identity crimes.

Violators face fines and/or imprisonment for producing or transferring false identification documents.

Experts encourage people to be proactive in taking steps to prevent and discover identity theft. Clearly, keeping it from happening in the first place is far less stressful than trying to resolve issues after identity theft crimes are committed. Here are a few of the things you can do to protect your personal financial information from identity theft criminals:

- Secure your personal information at all times. Don't leave lists of account numbers unlocked, and don't share your user IDs or passwords with ANYONE. Maintain as much control over your personal financial information as you can.

- Don't throw mail away if in contains any personal information, including your full name and address. Shred these documents before putting them in the garbage.

- Educate yourself about the techniques and tactics used in identity theft and protect yourself accordingly.

- Don't share personal account information with anyone, including co-workers, friends, and roommates. Unless they are also responsible for paying your bills, they have no reason to have this information. And don't give them your passwords without a very good reason. If you do share your passwords, change them as soon as possible.

- Shred unwanted and pre-approved credit applications, and have your name removed from those mailing lists.

- Be careful when you make purchases online to use only secure servers and to carefully guard your information. Do not keep a written list of passwords, and use passwords that are difficult to figure out (rather than something simple like your phone number).

This Product Is Brought To You By

Made in the USA
Lexington, KY
13 October 2012